# The Years of Ripening

# The Years of Ripening

## *Reflections on Aging in the Later Years*

Joyce Rupp

Maryknoll, New York 10545

Third Printing, April 2026

Founded in 1970, Orbis Books endeavors to publish works that enlighten the mind, nourish the spirit, and challenge the conscience. The publishing arm of the Maryknoll Fathers and Brothers, Orbis seeks to explore the global dimensions of the Christian faith and mission, to invite dialogue with diverse cultures and religious traditions, and to serve the cause of reconciliation and peace. The books published reflect the views of their authors and do not represent the official position of the Maryknoll Society. To learn more about Maryknoll and Orbis Books, please visit our website at www.orbisbooks.com.

---



Published by Orbis Books, Box 302, Maryknoll, NY 10545-0302.


Manufactured in the United States of America

---

Library of Congress Cataloging-in-Publication Data

Names: Rupp, Joyce, author.
Title: The years of ripening : reflections on aging in the later years / Joyce Rupp.
Description: Maryknoll, NY : Orbis Books, [2025] | Summary: "A companion volume to Vessels of Love, spiritual reflections on aging"-- Provided by publisher.
Identifiers: LCCN 2025005071 (print) | LCCN 2025005072 (ebook) | ISBN 9781626986381 (trade paperback) | ISBN 9798888660935 (epub)
Subjects: LCSH: Older people--Religious life. | Aging--Religious aspects---Christianity. | Christian life.
Classification: LCC BV4580 .R87 2025 (print) | LCC BV4580 (ebook) | DDC
248.8/5--dc23/eng20250505
LC record available at https://lccn.loc.gov/2025005071
LC ebook record available at https://lccn.loc.gov/2025005072

*For*
*the Elderhood Explorers*
*whose wisdom and openness*
*allowed me to learn from*
*their experience of aging*

*and*

*for all women and men*
*in their last decades of life*
*whose inherent goodness*
*continues to ripen*

# Contents

# Introduction

## "Now I Become Myself"

*The thing you are ripening toward*
*is the fruit of your life.*
*It will make you bright inside,*
*no matter what you are outside.*
*It is a shining thing.*

~ Helen Nearing

By the time we reach our eighth decade we will have entered the stage of life known as Elderhood, the last portion of life where we engage with the ripening of our spiritual orchard. Throughout our past, we seeded and grew our positive qualities. Now, in old age, we complete what still needs maturation, while rejoicing over the sweet taste of what has already been gathered into the harvest. We have the graced time and spacious presence to reflect, integrate, and bring to wholeness the significant features of our individual transformation that were previously set aside or not given enough attention.

The well-known lines in one of Robert Frost's poems,

But I have promises to keep,
And miles to go before I sleep,

are relevant in midlife but lose their potency when we reach eighty years. Now every day counts as never before. The reality of the road's ending looms closer. Our miles are no longer limitless. A lot of promises have been kept. Even if we live to be a hundred and five, the years will fly by quickly. So little time left. Now that I am in my early eighties, this thought does not produce dread. Rather, it creates a desire to live each day with a passion for living and increased spiritual attentiveness.

In the past, I lacked a thorough perception of what stirred within my deeper self because I was constantly rushing and pressing forward with the next thing to be accomplished on the "to do" list, intent on activating my fullest potential. But now my aged body will not allow hurrying. Neither will my mind. Both insist on slowing down. Consequently, the journey I am making as an elder has moved from a focus on the exterior realm of productivity to the interior realm of a contented presence. My urge to "do" has given way to a yearning to "be." I gain inner freedom as I release the "might do, could do, should do, and didn't do" insisting and scolding in the strained voice of my ego.

As you may have surmised by now, this book does not address issues of aging such as financial management, residential options, living wills, and medical insurance. *The Years of Ripening* focuses on personal transformation, the wonder and goodness of our hidden self, how the qualities of our personhood have been expressed, and in what ways we can claim ever more of the truest reality of our inner being. May Sarton's poetic verses in "Now I Become Myself" speak to this late-life occurrence. Her perception inspires me to live the quiet grandeur of the elder years, to rejoice in the song of myself, and to gladly tend to the aspects of core goodness that await their completion.

> Now I become myself. It's taken
> Time, many years and places;
> I have been dissolved and shaken,
> Worn other people's faces,
> Run madly, as if Time were there,
> Terribly old, crying a warning,
> "Hurry, you will be dead before _____"
> . . .
> As slowly as the ripening fruit
> Fertile, detached, and always spent,
> Falls but does not exhaust the root,
> So all the poem is, can give,
> Grows in me to become the song,
> Made so and rooted so by love.

The developments in Elderhood provide yeasty occasions to become our clearest self. As old age takes place, our physical being naturally weakens and wrinkles. At the same time, our non-physical being smooths out with a peaceful satisfaction. The tight ridges of past failures recede and dark illusions fade as we increasingly trust our life to be a harmonious song "rooted so by love." This encourages us to shed our self-willed, false control until we become freed from what binds our spirit. We let go of who we imagined ourselves to be and grow in a transparency that reveals our seasoned-with-love self.

## *The Experience of Elderhood*

Several years ago I received a message from Olive, whom I'd never met. Her honesty shook loose any misgivings I had about addressing the journey of elders. "I have your book on what you learned from your mother's aging (*Fly While You Still Have Wings*)," she wrote, "but now that I've turned ninety I need you to write one on very old age and its challenges—and I have to say, its scariness." Olive's message reminded me to avoid having this book be the type that urges "you can do anything at any age if you just give yourself to it." I've learned from those in their eighties and nineties that it's not a cheerleading voice they need to hear but a compassionate one. One that understands diminishment and decline, which is not to dismiss the joys and fulfilments inherent in old age.

I'm aiming for a presentation of what is great and not so great about Elderhood. Certain researchers and authors tend to depict later life as "the golden years." Yes, aging does encompass that, but it also includes corroded silver, rusty bronze, and chipped paint. Ask any older woman whose beloved spouse of five decades is now deceased, or a ninety-eight-year old whose severe arthritis confines him to a wheelchair. They will remind you that the last decades involve not only gifts but also gashes.

Numerous books on the topic of "aging" exist, many of them with titles using terms such as *conscious aging, creative aging, successful aging, mindful aging, healthy aging.* Most of these resources pertain to persons in their sixties and seventies. While some of the particulars directed toward aging relate to the final quarter of life, much does not sufficiently address the increasing challenges that arise for a person eighty or older—the reality of death drawing much closer, a body definitely wearing out, fading energy, distractedness, inability to quickly recall details and names, continual downsizing of space and material items, fewer items (if any) on the bucket list, accumulating deaths of family members and friends, and medical issues rapidly increasing in size and seriousness.

Besides these undesirable features of the final years, numerous positive ones also emerge, including increased freedom to be one's self without concern for what others think and judge, little interest in the pressure to be professionally successful, easily recognizable joys, cherished memories, less need to "run around," clearer insight and growing wisdom, sufficient time to spend with those counted as dear, a more peaceful spirit, a waning passion to take on projects to fix the world, an ever growing list of reasons for gratefulness, matured perception of what is truly meaningful and worthwhile, and the wideness of love that keeps expanding.

Best of all, the older we become, the more opportunities we have to develop the full potential of our goodness. Because of our less hurried life, the roots of selfless love have the space to grow stronger, and the fruits of that love can ripen into their fullest, juiciest flavors. Like other aged persons, I desire to strengthen this part of my being, to allow my inherent virtues to develop further. I do not want to miss a single piece of this precious life while trusting I can positively affect others by being a compassionate presence.

*Elderhood Explorers*

A year or so before poet Stanley Kunitz died at the age of one hundred, he spoke about getting back to writing after having been seriously ill: "I feel as though I am a traveler exploring territory that may not be wholly new, but it has reverberations and images that seem to have a collective presence. I don't know exactly where I am at this moment, in terms of the imaginative, creative process, but I know I am searching for something different from the terrain I was familiar with. . . . When I finally come to grips with my night vision, I'll know more clearly what it is I have in mind." A bit later in *The Wild Braid* Kunitz adds, "There seems to be a transformation going on in which I have a sense of a new life that I'm possessing. That I am not at all lost. I feel I have found myself, my strength. And I feel in possession of my destiny, not a victim of it."

I found the clarity and hope that Stanley Kunitz described regarding his inner exploration and future death to be a part of the lives of a group of women from age ninety to ninety-seven. When I first invited these members of my religious community to meet monthly, I proposed we name our gatherings "The Elderhood Explorers," describing my vision of our time together as "one of searching for deeper meaning, continued spiritual growth, and firmer peace in the ripening stage of Elderhood." I based this approach on a statement that Kathleen Dowling Singh makes in *The Grace of Aging*: "Aging can offer us the time to deliberately reorient ourselves toward the inner life, an infinitely more reliable refuge than anything the world can offer."

During the four years that we met, the elders' perceptive minds stayed open and attentive, even though their bodies grew increasingly frail. They would come into our gathering space using canes, wheelchairs, and walkers. Few managed to be free from those necessary aids. The sisters did not always immediately conjure up a detail from memory but they were fully alert to the content of the books and articles we discussed. They amazed me with how open, curious, and engaged they were in exploring their old age.

I also felt humbled by the sisters' honesty regarding how aging personally affected them. They awakened my understanding of late-life processes in countless ways, particularly in seeing how they differed from my then quite-active mid-seventies. Here are some comments I heard: "I don't think about hope so much as it is a time to rest." (At ease with slowing down.) "The things that used to be so important don't matter that much anymore." (Willingness to let go of what was once valued.) "God doesn't expect me to be perfect." (Acceptance of one's honest self.) "I've always had somebody to pull me out of the hole." (Gratitude for people who helped in the past and trusting someone to be there in the future.) "It takes me longer and longer to get dressed in the morning." (Progressive physical impairment.)

While I met with this group, I began delving into dozens of books and websites about aging. When the time drew near to begin writing *The Years of Ripening*, I also invited three dozen men and women to either respond to a written questionnaire or be personally interviewed about their approach to the final years. In contacting them, I sought confirmation of the topics relating to older persons that I planned to include. Their responses assured me that

I was on the right track. Since then, I've also received emails in which elders tell me of their situations. Some of these (whose names I've changed) are quoted with their permission in various essays. Each one corroborates my intuition and gleaned awareness that Elderhood deserves to be given as much attention as any of the earlier stages of adult development.

### *About This Book*

*The Years of Ripening* does not approach aging as a right or wrong way to live. It is not my intent to lump older persons into one category by contending that the characteristics of Elderhood are true for every person. Each one has his or her own family history, individual personality, health condition, and life experience. No two persons manage to grow old in exactly the same manner. Some require assistance with ordinary tasks long before they are eighty, and others retain their adeptness at self and home care far into their nineties. Yet, commonalities do exist, enough to allow for a strong sense of kinship with other people making their way along the ever-changing route of Elderhood.

The contents of this book relate to the profound transition of personal transformation that takes place in old age, one in which death's insistent whisper in us becomes louder. We learn how to be at peace with who we are and how we are as we gradually accept the third stage of aging, which Hindu wisdom terms that of "the forest dweller." As we embrace the inward focus coming from this slowing down mode and trust the value of being a loving presence, we eventually slide into the final stage of adult transformation known as that of "the renunciate." This is when elders pare down to the bare minimum, oftentimes becoming immobile and reliant on others for a good portion of self-care. As renunciates, we either choose to release our attachments, (both material and non-material), or they are wrenched from us by such things as ill health and cognitive impairment. This final stage signifies harvesting—like the dried husk of an ear of corn torn off to reveal the golden sustenance inside, or the shell of a walnut being cracked open so the nutrients can be retrieved. In this stripping down to the bare essentials, we gain what truly counts: an inner self overflowing with an abundance of ripened love available to those who enter our lives.

I invite you to walk into the orchard of Elderhood. *Your* orchard. Consider the valuable history found there. Taste the texture of your vast experience. Let the nectar of transparent love flow into and out of your heart. Welcome with grateful gladness the wonder of who you have been and are today. Enjoy your ripening spirit. Ready yourself for the final harvest.

If we approach our last years as an opportunity to bring the harvest to fruition, we will have aged well. We will have given a precious gift to those close to us and to the larger world as we freely offer the gift of the person we are, the one we have come to know, accept, and value. We will be like the father in Anchee Nin's *Pearl of China*, living peacefully until we depart.

> A week later, Papa stopped breathing.
> Like a ripe melon, Papa hung happily on his vine
> before dropping to the ground.

All is not ended with our final departure. We leave behind the beauty and bounty that resided within our aged selves. Like a ripened melon on the vine, so the matured fruit of our loving heart and weathered wisdom leave a beneficial legacy to nurture a future generation.

# I

# A Time to Ripen

## "Birthday Come and Gone"

Another birthday. Come and gone.
What to make of the life left?
How to tend the unfinished past,
What to savor, what to let be?

Another birthday. Come and gone.
One day closer to the last breath.
More opportunities to enjoy life.
More time to ripen the truest love.

Another birthday. Come and gone.
Release desire for accomplishment.
Believe more fully in kindly presence.
Tap into jewels resting in the soul.

Go forward. Peacefully. Hopefully.
Go inward. Steadily. Faithfully.

Go outward. Lovingly. Tenderly.
Go slowly. Patiently. Sage-fully.

Dream more. Love more.
Hang around with nature.
Enjoy pleasures of the heart.
Nurture valued relationships.

Remain true to divine Wisdom,
Faithful Guide, Friend of the soul,
Partner of inner transformation,
Companion to the end. And beyond.

~ Joyce Rupp

# *Entering Elderhood*

*Listen to your life.*
*See it for the fathomless mystery that it is.*
*In the boredom and pain of it*
*no less than in the excitement and gladness;*
*touch, taste, smell your way to the holy*
*and hidden heart of it.*

~ Frederick Buechner

More than thirty years ago I met Sister Bernadette slowly making her way up the stairs. Always a private person, she rarely spoke about her personal thoughts and feelings. On this day, however, she paused on the stairs and surprised me with her open and exposed statement: "Today is my eightieth birthday. For the first time, I feel old." How I wish I had asked what led her to feel that way. But I was young and did not understand what she meant other than noticing she walked more slowly.

Now I understand. Being in Elderhood myself, I realize that no matter how young we feel inside—no matter how many or how few aches and pains—we eventually reach the surrendered point of admitting to the dimming of our years. If we're honest and alert, there comes a time when we look at ourselves and say, *I am old*. We know there aren't that many birthdays left for us here on Earth. Something within urges us to live our fullest and be our truest self—now or never. But when does that moment of sheer honesty arrive? When does *I am an old person* become our accepted reality?

Who can say when Elderhood or being old begins? Much depends on health of body, mind, and spirit, along with financial and relationship circumstances. Someone in our Elderhood Explorers group mentioned it was a heart attack in her late eighties that convinced her "the years were piling up." I began to sense a transition into this passage of life after my seventieth birthday. My physical health was still strong and I had a lot of energy. But I noticed an increasing weariness in the evenings and a grudging disposition about working full time. The once smooth skin on my face developed sneaky wrinkles and my brown hair began transitioning to white.

My biggest turn toward Elderhood, though, was not in the physical realm. This happened interiorly and was largely due to how the transitions of others affected my spirit. The number of people slipping from my life through illness and death increased significantly. More friends were selling the homes they'd lived in for forty or fifty years to move into townhouses and condos. Some had no choice but to enter assisted living. Others moved to a warmer climate or to be closer to family members. In still other cases I lost the person I knew due to their cognitive decline.

All these changes and more are parts of the Elderhood stage. The passageway of aging consists of a pilgrimage of the heart in which we look more intently at what stirs in the soul and begs for attention. As we tend to these aspects of self, our personal authenticity and peacefulness gradually ripen. While exterior aspects related to the physical body and to society influence this period of life, Elderhood is equally shaped by the inner self and what evolves there. The interior influences the exterior and vice versa, as Vincent Pizzuto acknowledges: "And as with all pilgrims, we must walk simultaneously in two directions: the exterior and the interior."

In Elderhood, the external world becomes the teacher of the deeper self and a superb catalyst for personal transformation. The inner world summons meaning to surface from those experiences. This is what the last decades open up more widely for older persons—keener insight and sharpened awareness about becoming a transparent and loving human being. When gracious elders die, they leave behind a world with more love in it than when they arrived.

While it is true that the later years of life are strewn with enriching and affirming aspects, they also reveal evidence of rusted-out components, frayed fragments, and a life that has lost its shine. If you are sixty or seventy, you may not agree with this, but if you are in your eighties or nineties, you'll undoubtedly be nodding your head "yes."

Elderhood presents an opportunity to make peace with the part of the self that balks at the limitations and relinquishments. Older age promises the prospect of inner serenity through recognizing and a coming to terms with certain elements of the personality or remnants of the past that hold us back from genuine, inner harmony. This late phase of life also requires an acceptance of human mortality. The final years ask us to recognize our own mortality and to accept it in a way that ensures a serene passing.

The reality of our eventual departure does not mean that our aging self lacks joy. Rather, attention to what is actually happening in our life brings a sense of completion and fulfillment. Our kinship with others of a similar age also strengthens us. Knowing we are not alone in what we experience encourages us to trust our resilience to live, not with resignation, but with contentment in accepting who we are and how we are. We still have significant living to do, albeit more from the inside than from the outside of ourselves.

In *The Inner Work of Age*, Connie Zweig titles her prologue "A Letter to My Fellow Travelers in Late Life." She offers a summary of hope for the ripening years: "You can discover how to reorient by turning within, attuning your soul's longing and cultivating a deeper shift in awareness. You can discover how to move through the passage of late life as a rite, releasing past forms, facing the unknown, and emerging as an Elder filled with vitality and purpose."

Our elder years do not lack for vitality and purpose. They invite us to be as fully immersed as possible in the wonder and goodness of our existence. The joys and sorrows, the good and not-so-good moments, the many experiences that shaped our personalities, the love that entered our hearts, the countless kindnesses and benefits we may have overlooked or sidestepped—all this we visit and integrate into the totality of who we are.

Each day of Elderhood we have the option of listening to our life, of continuing to become ever more in tune with the goodness and mystery of our personhood. Here we mine the treasures hidden in the ordinary everyday. We bask gratefully as we marvel at the life we have been given.

# *A Time to Ripen*

*The fourth quarter of each of our journeys*
*is a time of ripening.*
~ Kathleen Dowling Singh

When we entered this world at birth, our core self was full of possibilities. Our essence contained seeds of goodness—life-giving virtues, positive characteristics, altruistic qualities meant to be nurtured and cared for until they reached maturity and were ready for harvesting. These seeds have always been a part of us. Many of them have already developed and influenced the welfare of ourselves and others. Some qualities are growing closer to being ripened, while others may still require considerable growth.

Pomegranates remind me of the incredible amount of goodness available and ready to be revealed within persons of an older age. Each round, reddish pomegranate contains clusters of seeds. A single fruit might contain as many as two hundred to fourteen hundred seeds, which are known to be "rich in antioxidants, fiber, and vitamins." Imagine the possibilities for nourishment that one mature pomegranate produces. So, too, with us. The plentiful qualities in us contain tremendous potential, always more dimensions of goodness to grow, ripen, and harvest.

This has happened for me with the seed of compassion. Long did this quality remain dormant, waiting for me to deliberately give it my attention. I began to do this in my sixties, both by learning about compassion's many facets and by putting it into practice in my thoughts and actions. When I was in my twenties, if someone had suggested that I contained the possibility for compassion, my understanding of this virtue would have been narrow, surfacy, and limited. I had not lived long enough nor had I experienced sufficient suffering to comprehend compassion's true nature. But in late life I have an endless stream of lived experiences. There's now much soul-soil in which to grow and tend this virtue. The more I focus on it, the more I discover how much compassion requires of me. Thus, with the passage of time, my ability to be compassionate has expanded and deepened.

In *Anam Cara*, John O'Donohue describes the interior process of aging this way: "As your body ages and gets weaker, your soul is in fact getting richer, deeper, and stronger. With time your soul grows more sure of itself; the natural light within it increases and brightens." How I wish we had glimpses of the soul's radiance. If only a curtain were pulled aside so we could see how the inner life evolves and becomes ever more luminous.

In a way, this curtain *is* drawn aside from time to time. There are certain older people whose luminous quality of presence attracts us. We might not be able to name what it is that draws us to be near them to receive a touch of their transparent authenticity. But when we are with them, we sense a gracious acceptance of the person we are. We dwell in the beauty of their light-filled, ripening presence.

I've been with older people whose inner light shines through their countenance. I've felt peaceful in their presence because of their serenity. I recall an older member of our community who came across as crotchety. I learned to be on guard when around her because of her caustic comments and her chronic attitude of irritation, which was probably due to arthritic pain rarely kept at bay. As this cantankerous woman grew older, the sharp comments gradually ceased. What happened within her as she aged I do not know, but the transformation was evident. Her eyes glowed with love, sparkled with a quiet joy. The seed of equanimity had obviously matured and I found myself enjoying any opportunity to visit with her.

The inner growth of our virtues happens much like that of fruit, which requires the energy of sun, water, and nutritious soil. We are continually urged toward fullness by an unseen spiritual power greater than the forces of nature that energize the hormone ethylene that activates the ripening in fruit. These exterior elements of nature are crucial, just as the external aspects of our life are in affecting personal growth. They reach into the secluded heart of our hidden being and influence the maturation of our truest self.

The poet Rainer Maria Rilke refers to this energy in *The Book of Hours*:

> My looking ripens things
> and they come toward me, to meet and be met.

Rilke precedes this by referring to a "power" within himself that helps to "give shape" to his world. This power lies in his "beholding" of things, implying a gaze of reverent attentiveness. The way he sees changes the way he looks at life. Thus, his experience becomes more meaningful. When we behold our life, instead of just putting up with it, we find within it a source of empowerment for further development of our attributes and a confirmation of their maturing presence.

As much as we'd like it to be otherwise, we cannot hurry or force this fruition. We can only give ourselves prayerfully and intentionally to it. Some of us have a tendency to look at others our age and judge how certain qualities have grown much faster and more thoroughly for them than for us. When I was on retreat in the Sonoran Desert, I saw a prickly pear cactus with two splendid yellow flowers at least a month after all the rest of the cacti had cheered the land with their colors. Those two late bloomers caught my full attention in a way they never would have in the glory of the earlier blooming season. They stood out and brought me much needed joy. These two yellow flowers blooming late in the season were reminiscent of the voices of older people who tell me, with sadness, blame, guilt, or apology, that they don't understand why their spiritual awakening took so long, why it still needs more attention. They fail to grasp how splendid the late-in-life blooming of our virtues can be.

In *The Grace of Living* Kathleen Dowling Singh remarks, "Outwardly and expressively it may look quite different for each of us. The ripening pours through our unique individuality. Inwardly, in inner and secret ways, the realized awareness of ripening is of the same taste—liberation. . . . I think of the many who have returned to their own playfulness, their own original ease."

So whether this freedom and authenticity arrive early or late, what counts is that we are capable of our ripening and giving ourselves to this process. Buddhist monk Thich Nhat Hanh reminded his followers that "Anything good needs time to ripen." Like the later blooming of the prickly pear cactus, it is never too late for our latent virtues to flourish.

# *Don't Call Me Old*

*Don't call me old. Call me awakening.*

~ Marsha Sinetar

Five women with slow gaits and white hair left a local restaurant and crossed the street in front of my car as I waited for the red signal light to change. One used a cane, the rest meandered leisurely, talking and laughing with a spirit of lightheartedness. They looked happy and unstressed at that moment, but my eighty-year-old inner voice snarled, "I don't want to be one of *them.*" I was quite taken aback by that negative reaction. I thought about it the rest of the way home. On the following days that snarl wouldn't leave me alone, not until I faced the truth of my inner ageist.

This awakening came about at the Perk-Up Cafe where I was to meet a couple my age for lunch. I arrived early, looked around for my friends (who had not yet arrived) and was appalled at the number of casually dressed customers who looked a bit frumpy, women with no makeup and most of the men overweight. There was even a woman with a black hairpiece flopped sideways on top of her thinning, gray hair. As I stood there judging the people, it dawned on me: *I am one of them. It's not a "me and them" anymore. I am like some of "the old people" here.*

Ageism operates in several ways: It's how younger people in our Western society tend to gauge the value of those in late life, usually judging these people as dismissible and having little merit. Ageism also persists in older adults themselves when their inner orientation refuses to accept the reality of their present stage of life. They deny or refuse to accept their oldness, insisting on thinking, acting, and looking much younger than they actually are.

Our inner ageist exists in a variety of ways, such as Vera exhibited in her mid-eighties. She constantly criticized people her age in the retirement center and associated only with people at least ten years younger than herself. Vera's clothes and language reflected her attempts to disguise her age, a refusal to accept and enjoy being her authentic self. Consequently, she suffered from anxiety attacks and was rarely content, continually complaining about not being accepted, not being appreciated.

Sometimes how we view our aging self comes through in more subtle ways. When she was in her late seventies, my aunt Jean enjoyed adventurous trips by bus with other retired travelers. Jean told me about a flamboyant woman who often went on those same outings. She would tell people she was ninety although she was actually eighty. Thus, the other travelers marveled at how young she looked and how spry she was "for her age."

When Connie Zweig writes about ageism, she describes it this way:

> With ageism, we project our negative fantasies of "old"—ugly, frail, needy, senile—which leads to condescension and stereotyping: greedy geezer, old bat, over the hill, out to pasture. And when millions of

> people project what they fear about aging onto elders, the latter try to appear and act as if they are younger. Hence the epidemic of anti-aging marketing, advertising, surgery, and hormone replacement therapy. Further, as our society as a whole—young people, old people, and everyone in between—buys into a stereotype that devalues Elders, as well as our lifetimes of skill and wisdom, a collective inner agism takes over.

On the day the older women crossed the street, I experienced both of those aspects—seeing them as old and separating myself from their age. That view developed out of the way I knew society assessed me. I actually enjoy life, and I consider myself fortunate to have lived to reach my eighth decade. I have no quarrels with most of my aging process. When my inner voice resounds with "I hate being old," it's not because of who and how I am but because of how I experience being viewed by others—just an old lady—feeble, invisible, insignificant, and not counting for much.

Many is the time when I've been spoken to as an irrelevant, older person. One day as I put my key in the outside door to the apartment building, I heard people coming down the stairs. I stood back and held the door open for a dad carrying a small girl and another one walking behind him. Just before they passed through the door I heard the older girl say to him, "It's just a gramma." I didn't mind "gramma." After all, I *am* of that vintage. What I did linger on was the word "just." Did this mean "harmless" or "of no concern?" I'll never know, but the word reminded me of how much of society views older people as being irrelevant.

This began happening to me when I was in my early sixties and still traveling to lead workshops and retreats. In one place, the coordinator of the event (maybe ten years younger than I was) asked me if I needed a stool to get onto the platform that was only ten inches higher than the floor. To add to that insult, she then inquired if I needed a golf cart to get to the lecture hall, which was only a four-minute walk away.

I never minded being called "ma'am" by airport gate agents, but I felt offended one day when I went to board a plane to travel for work. I stood in a line with businessmen who, like me, were well-traveled and had early seating preference. The agent in her forties looked at me. "Need extra time?" she asked with too much sweetness, indicating that she thought the only reason for my being in that line was that I was an older, white-haired woman. I felt humiliated by her misperception. Being seen as useless, ignored, overlooked, or spoken to in a demeaning manner has increased my empathy for refugees, immigrants, people of color, low-income residents, and homeless persons, all of whom are also ignored, unaccepted, or seen as a blight on society's landscape. When I am treated as "a little old lady," I have a sense of how they must feel.

Comments that are meant to be positive belittle older people: "I can't believe you're ninety-two. You look so good for your age." "You'd never know you're eighty-six. You're so spry." "How do you manage to have so few wrinkles?" "What's your secret for staying young?"

Due to our society's view of old age, each of us probably harbors some ageism in how we see ourselves or other aged persons. We don't need to chide ourselves about this. It would be helpful, though, if we could look at one another with the sincere belief that each person in the later years contains treasures of great price—worth much more than all the flawless skin in the world.

# *Looking Good*

*It's such a nuisance that elderly people have to look so old.*

~ Annie Lyons

When my friend and I go out for dinner every couple of months we can count on having a laugh if the wait-person who comes to our table appears a to be lot younger than our early eighties. He or she will inquire what we might like to drink. This question quickly follows with suggestions, such as, "Iced tea or one of our specialty-flavored, non-alcoholic beverages?" What fun to see the barely concealed surprise on the wait-person's face when we give our order for a vodka gimlet and a scotch-on-the-rocks.

Younger persons have all sorts of assumptions about older people, just as we older persons have assumptions about younger ones, so I try to take this particular sort of condescension with relative ease (most of the time). When I had a colonoscopy, the attending physician was late. The nurse who chose to stay with me placed his hand gently on my arm and spoke to me the entire forty-five minutes I waited. I didn't ask him to stay with me, nor did I need him to be there. I understood he was being compassionate, presuming I was fearful because I was in my mid-seventies and had white hair. I was not scared. I actually felt calm, but his kindness touched me and I easily accepted his treating me as if I were an anxious woman of advanced years.

Other incidents are not as pleasant. Strangers speak extra loud, even though we can hear just fine. Then there are the ones who presume we are unable to perform tasks similar to theirs. I was sixty when the hostess where I was staying (she was probably in her early forties, someone I did not know) asked me if I could get my legs over the side of the bathtub in order to take a shower. I felt insulted, assured her I walked three miles every day and was in excellent health. I wonder what she would say to me now that I'm twenty years older, and I can *still* get my legs over the side of the bathtub.

Younger people caution, "Are you sure you can manage that?" when I'm carrying a bag of groceries. My response is usually, "Thank you. I'm stronger than I look." When I do need assistance with carrying something, I'll gladly accept it, but please, don't think I'm incapable of carrying a small bag of groceries.

I was walking joyfully at my best speed on the bike path around the prairie when a young woman on a bike approached me. In passing she turned her head toward me and called "You're doing a great job." That comment immediately snagged my joy. I thought, "She'd never say that to a husky male biker or a peer of hers, so why did she think it necessary to say it to me?" She meant well but her words implied "Wow, you're walking fast for someone so ancient."

I feel a similar irritation when total strangers call me "sweetie pie," "honey," or "dear." Would they call someone much younger by those names? I feel especially rankled when some older guy thinks he's being nice by greeting me with, "Hello, young lady."

I've been patronizing, too. I once boarded a plane with my frisky, fifty-year-old self ready to fly to where I was speaking that weekend. When I found my assigned seat, there was what I considered an old woman sitting by the window. She looked a bit like a ladybug slouched in her seat—a round, extended tummy, skinny arms and legs, a dear face. I greeted her with "Good morning." After getting settled in my seat, I turned and asked about her destination. I then asked, "Going to visit grandchildren?" She gave me one of those "stuff it, lady" smiles and replied, "No, I'm going to join my family on the Boundary Waters in the northern part of the state." Well, that quickly put me in my place. Being on the wilderness *Boundary Waters* is no easy task with its canoeing, portaging, and camping. Now that I'm her age, I realize what a snippy approach I took with this woman.

Pope Francis named it well when he jokingly commented to a Telemundo Network journalist, "People tell us 'You look good.' That's what they say to old people." No doubt they intend to have us not feel as old as we look—even though we do look as old as we are. So what ought people say when they meet us?—perhaps "I'm happy to see you again." or "How is life treating you?"

In his *New York Times* article, "Out the Window: The View in Winter," national poet laureate Donald Hall muses on how even though a certain response to an aged person "might be good-hearted," it can be unintentionally disdainful. He gives the example of someone writing an affirming note about him in a local newspaper. "She calls me *a nice old gentleman*. She intends to praise me, with *nice* and *gentleman*. 'Old' is true enough, and she lets us know that I am not a grumpy old fart, but *nice* and *gentleman* put me in a box where she can rub my head and hear me purr."

This type of judgmental and inadvertent condescension can be dismissed, but there are other forms that ought not be tolerated. In another experience, Donald Hall describes being in the *National Gallery of Art* with a friend who pushes him in a wheelchair as they view the exhibits. A guard saunters by and asks if they know the sculptor's name. Before they can respond, the guard tells them. Hall says nothing even though he has written an entire book about that particular sculptor. The poet ignores this indirect put-down, but he cannot and ought not tolerate what happens with the guard a couple of hours later: "We emerge from the cafeteria and see the same man, who asks Linda if she enjoyed her lunch. Then he bends over to address me, wags his finger, smiles a grotesque smile, and raises his voice to ask, "Did we have a nice din-din?"

When this sort of ignorant deference takes place, it's time to stand up for ourselves and make it known that we are not babies. At moments like this, we inform the speaker by acknowledging how loathsome their tone of voice and words are to us: "Would you want to be spoken of in that way? I am an adult. Please address me like the intelligent person I am. Your baby-talk insults me."

Sometimes we can be too nice or too accepting of the way we are treated as older persons. If society is going to be more knowledgeable of what being spoken to condescendingly feels like, we will have to let them know the disrespect it indicates. Otherwise, they will keep on speaking and acting in a patronizing way.

II

# Anxiety and Uncertainty

## "Resistances and Fears"

They leap into the mind
like over-sexed frogs
croaking for a partner,
alluring, convincing.

Fears and resistances,
bold refusals to climb out
of the comfy home schedule,
dread of the ever-unknown,
disturbed by risky challenges
that may never materialize.

Do the seeds for inner growth
reside within this anxious spirit?

What is best for the soul,
the body, the mind?

What in one's little buried world
cries out to be stretched
beyond resolute bondage?

The answer hides itself
while the heart strains to find it.

When I listen, I know.

When I know, I step beyond
what tries its utmost
to hold me back.

~ Joyce Rupp

# *If Rather than When*

*The world may be full of "retirement plans,"*
*but who can really plan much? And be sure of it?*
*Life is not a straight line, we learn.*
*It is, if anything, a spiral.*

~ Joan Chittister

Our vocabulary changes as we age. We know we have fewer years before us than we had in the past and that the body naturally declines. Having moved quite a distance past retirement, our conversations certainly tend to include more medical verbiage. There is also one word that almost always replaces another in the accumulating years. "When" gets ditched and "If" becomes dominant. Use of this two letter word grows more frequent with the realization that death draws closer as good health becomes less certain.

In her eighties my mother stopped planning very far ahead. "Let's wait and see," she'd say. When she first responded this way, I thought, "Wait for what?" Gradually I understood. She meant "wait to see *if* I am still alive, *if* I am mobile enough, *if* I have the energy to do what you're suggesting." I didn't like hearing my mother's indecision because it drew me too close to the truth of her weakening health and eventual departure. Her death was not something I wanted to befriend. Now that I'm catapulting into the final stretch, I understand all too well what my mother inferred with that ominous *If*.

That two letter proviso keeps me mindful that my life may quickly change, that I am not totally in charge of it, even if I'd like to be or think I am. "If" encourages me to be humble and keep my persistent ego from thinking I can force what I insist on doing. "If" slows me down and whispers valuable advice, "Don't look too far ahead. Take a happy look at what is here today." Accepting the conditional "If" enables me to keep my eye on what is of greatest importance now.

Uncertainty stalks the rim of every human life, whether there's awareness of it or not. For the older person, ambiguity regularly inserts itself. Questions without answers leave a trail of unknowns: What part of the body will cooperate or balk, maybe even threaten to quit altogether? Will emptiness of heart spread loneliness further? Will there be news today about another friend being seriously ill or having died? How long will it take to get dressed? Is it possible to get shoes on swollen feet? Is the lack of remembering details normal? Will a stroke, a heart attack, or a brain bleed end life as I know it? Will a sudden fall result in a broken hip or pelvis, possibly making the comfort of home a thing of the past?

There is, of course, a necessary balance between "living in the now" and "planning for the future." While our mind can get caught up in thinking too far ahead, we also have to look at basic considerations regarding what could possibly happen (such as moving from our current residence into assisted living or full-time care). Once we detect and delineate these plans, we can let the details sit by the sidelines until the time arrives for full attention.

One day my friend Bob, who is in his early-nineties, quipped, "I don't buy green bananas anymore." He's a gregarious individual who continually discovers new friends and makes a deliberate effort to enjoy every day that he's alive. I've observed how he doesn't let "if" keep him from enjoying life, how he deliberately sets aside anxious thoughts that try to gnaw their way in. When Bob feels depressed, he reaches out to those he counts on for support. When he lacks physical energy he still goes for a daily walk, maybe going slower and not as far. He does do some planning, like scheduling medical appointments and regularly checking with his financial consultant, but he doesn't sit in the bathtub of "what if" all day and let his spirit get waterlogged and crinkly.

At a gathering of friends not long ago, we were invited to reflect on ourselves as being pilgrims on a journey—to consider what this might be like for us. My mind immediately wandered back to twenty years earlier when I learned about "if." At age sixty, I was an actual pilgrim trekking four hundred fifty miles across northern Spain with the goal of ending at the cathedral of St. James in Santiago. That is how I learned about being at peace with "if." Had I not done so, I would have been engulfed in the uncertainty of each day and missed the wonder of the transformative experience in the walk itself.

During that pilgrimage so little was known as I started out each morning—I wasn't sure where I would find food or what I would eat, where I'd be staying, how the weather might be, if my health and that of my walking partner could be maintained, or what the landscape ahead would be like. I'm hardly a pilgrim like that now, with the security of a mobile phone, an assured residence, a calendar displaying my schedule, a refrigerator full of food, and easy access to daily weather forecasts. Having all this, I convince myself of certainty—even though this belief is false because everything eventually changes.

We are all pilgrims in spirit, journeying through life and never more so than during Elderhood. Most of us elders move onward in our daily existence without being overly occupied with the unknowns, but we do realize there's not much certainty about anything except our mortality. We have to decide how to live with the obscurities and not let them overpower our mind or reach their talons into the crevices of our heart. There are definitely times when I'm full of questions about who I am becoming. I learn over and over how to let the *will there, what if*, and *maybe* sit on the sidelines. Without denying the uncertainties, I trust that satisfaction can be found each day, that the future will move me smoothly forward if I do not demand a lot of definite answers from it.

The goal of the older pilgrim is not to arrive at a cathedral in Spain but to be transformed into the fullness of love. There are countless ways for this to take place. Choosing to be at peace with "if" and maintaining an untroubled spirit about "when" can be one of those ways.

# *Just Do It*

*I told myself that the older we get,*
*the more life invites us to hold fear*
*with compassion and gentleness.*

~ Jennifer Jinks Hoffmann

Just do it!" That was Jon's matter-of-fact response after I voiced my hesitations about being seventy-eight and spending two weeks of solitude in a winter cabin for some uninterrupted writing time. My friend's rejoinder was exactly what I needed to get me out of the rut of fearing, "What if I can't cope with the long nights of darkness and frigid cold? Will I get bored or snowed in for days with no electricity? What if I feel depressed and have no desire to write?"

The next day, after being with Jon, I booked the state park cabin. I absolutely loved my time there in late January. In the following years I've gone back to the same place for another two weeks in winter. They are just as marvelous as the previous ones. How much I would have missed had I given in to those pushy concerns.

Everyone experiences trepidation at certain times. The honest and wise poet, Nikki Giovanni, begins her poem, "Vegetable Soup" with two short lines:

I think I'm afraid
of growing old.

For some, the thought of growing old leads to anxiety-ridden apprehensions. Some common ones include: being alone, becoming a burden, having acute pain, being forgotten, wondering "what will become of me," losing control of bodily functions, not being able to drive, the death of a loved one, facing one's own dying, living with financial insecurity, becoming dependent and vulnerable, a fall resulting in permanent immobility, or residing in a nursing home.

In her website article "Insights about Aging," Gina Lake presents valuable questions for elders to consider:

> The fear of aging is another fear about the future that haunts many. What meaning do you give to the idea of aging? What beliefs do you have around it? What do you assume about it? Will it make you ugly? Weak? Unlovable? Does it mean you'll be unhappy? Have a miserable existence? Unable to do things? Cast aside? Worthless? These ideas are all unreal, untrue concepts.

Some older persons refuse to consider leaving the home they've lived in for decades, even though they can no longer manage the upkeep or muster the energy to cook healthy meals. They conjure up the worst scenarios about what living elsewhere might be like, failing to consider what advantages could result by making the move. When we stop risking and refuse to go beyond our comfort zone, this lack of venturing into the unknown gradually floods over into other arenas of life—staying home instead of attending social gatherings, losing interest in what's going on in the larger world, or giving up efforts to maintain our health.

"Fear is a mood to be moved through, not a voice to be obeyed" writes Mark Nepo in *The Book of Soul.* Fear can wield an unbelievable amount of influence by leading us astray and stealing our happiness. While it can sometimes be a friend instead of a foe when it warns of danger or protects us from harm, mostly it does more damage than good, especially when it affects making choices and decisions about how to live. If elders allow that voice to become a tyrant, it will seek to control their lives.

The authors of *Wise Aging* remind us "As we anticipate the losses and the pain of old age, our imagination is fertile. . . . Fear may feel very palpable, but we need to move through it to discover what may be on the other side." Until we arrive at that "other side," or begin to move toward it, we can join with other elders in addressing our concerns about what might happen to us in the future.

What a difference it makes when we face our trepidations and go beyond them. When my colleague Steve looked back on his open-heart surgery last year, he discovered what awaited him *on the other side.* He remarked, "I feel better now than I have in a long time." I admired Steve for taking the risk and being willing to give himself vulnerably to the medical people who could improve his health. What if he had succumbed to a persistent fear and never gone ahead with the surgery?

When fear enters our mind, it threatens to dissolve our peace. It can be helpful to have a talk with our fear, to ask how it arrived and what it wants from us. Acknowledgment of this internal terrorizer eases its subtle power to take over our inner atmosphere. When we pause to listen to what clamors for our attention internally, we begin to take charge of it. For instance, I might say to my anxiousness about falling, "Yes, I am more wobbly on my feet than I used to be. I know I must be alert to where and how I walk, and to wear reliable shoes. Now that you've helped me be conscious of this, I won't need you to keep nagging about it. I still intend to go to the family reunion."

If this insistent cache of dread and concern grows into a giant size, we may have to do some negotiating, give it fifteen minutes of our time each day, but no more. If this determined visitor insists on shoving its way in for more time than that, we say to the whiney voice, "No. I've allowed you the attention you can have for today. I'm not going to listen to you. Stop pestering me." If that approach does not lessen the uneasiness, we can go back in memory to other times when we were filled with concern over something that never materialized. We'll notice how much of our precious internal time and peace was tossed away needlessly because of it.

Unnecessary and excessive fear suffocates the spirit. We can be so determined to protect our well-being that we end up having nothing but an iron-clad, safeguarded existence. Fear has the power to have us die long before we die. It can paralyze and immobilize the pulse of joy and warp our outlook on life. In Elderhood, we refuse to allow this invasive emotion to destroy our zest for living. We choose, instead, to be curious, to be open to both the possibilities and the uncertainties that live within the unknown.

# *Worrying*

*You don't have forever, so why worry*
*about things you cannot change?*

~ Nancy Wood

Fear leads to worrying. Meditation teacher Tryshe Dhevney knows that "thoughts are as powerful as words." When worrying entrenches itself in our thinking, it can snip apart our inner sanctum of peace and toss it out to the vultures of anxiety to devour. Worry writes in big letters with indelible ink, suggesting endless possibilities of what could possibly be detrimental—predicting lots of doom and gloom. Worrying nags at us about what to expect, the dire consequences, upsetting results—whether these be about financial matters, medical tests, illness of loved ones, how to resolve differences with a longtime friend, or other issues that batter us around. These anxious thoughts keep us from having a positive disposition or a good night's sleep. Trish Herbert reminds her readers in *Journeywell*: "It takes a conscious and mighty effort for some of us to see the positive side of things."

Worrying throws us inside a cogwheel of turbulence. Round and round we go, growing more weary and unfocused with each circular mental turning. One of my dear friends often referred to this as "fretting." She would get caught up in whether or not she could manage what she had promised to do, or thought she had to accomplish. Small things would loom larger and larger. The more she dwelt on them, the more emotionally numbed she felt, until she would be unable to get herself to follow through on much of anything.

I've never considered myself a big worrier. I like to think I have a hopeful outlook on most situations. But since I've gotten older, the useless tirade of thoughts that elicits the futile emotion of worry seems to be creeping in more often. Or maybe it's that I am more aware of what goes on inside my mind because it's not filled with trying to meet the threatening work deadlines that used to dominate my overly full life.

One of these worrying times occurred when I entered my eighth decade. I wanted to rejoice in the wonder, goodness, and beauty of my life. I refused to approach turning eighty as the "black balloons" and "you're way over the hill" that tends to flavor birthdays of older people. About three months before my birthday, I made plans to throw a party for myself. I laughed about how ludicrous that seemed, but I also enjoyed the thought of having longtime friends and siblings come together for an evening of fun. How surprised I was that just a few weeks into planning I started worrying about highly unlikely catastrophes—be careful not to break a bone; watch out for other drivers so they don't crash my car; maybe there will be a storm that evening and the electricity will go off; I could get Covid again; the food caterer won't show up. The worry that finally led me out of that twisted thinking was the day I briefly choked on a salad. My first thought—"Oh, a great way to die before the party."

When I could breathe, I laughed. It was definitely time to get a hold on those pestering worries. I spoke directly to them, making sure they understood I was setting every one of them aside. I then wrote and repeated an affirmation each morning: *The birthday party is a success and goes wonderfully well.* The night of the gathering turned out to be "magical," as those present described it. The weather at the nature lodge allowed the lake to shimmer with a calming glow as the sun set. The jubilation and conversation among the group sparkled. The songs we joined in were filled with gusto. The food was delicious.

Most of my worries, though, are not about what will happen to me. They stem from concerns regarding those I care about, their health and well-being. I'm not alone in this. I often hear grandparents express worry about their grandchildren's lives. A partner in a longtime marriage becomes distraught by constantly considering what will happen to one of them when the other "goes first." I also sense anxiety in older people who speak about what our planet and our world will be like in the future, given the dismal, environmental news that abounds. If we're fortunate, we will have understanding persons to help us regain and keep our balance when our lethal worries get out of hand.

I've learned how helpful others can be when we're hesitant to do something and become anxious about it. After I gave my cross-country skis away because the arthritis in my hands had weakened them too much to use the poles, I didn't want to give up being in winter's wonderland. I bought some snowshoes on sale that spring but when the following winter arrived they sat in the closet, looking intimidating. I didn't know how to put them on and was concerned with how difficult it might be to walk with them. I wondered, too, if I would have enough strength in my legs to walk very far.

Then one day, after a beautiful, fresh snowfall, my friend Judy texted, "Want to snowshoe in Walnut Woods?" I almost responded "no" or made an excuse not to go. I was that worried about being able to accomplish the feat. But I chose, instead, to speak to her about my apprehension regarding how to use the snowshoes. "No problem," she wrote back. "I'll help you out."

When we met at the park, Judy was patient as I learned how to put the snowshoes on. Then away we went on the trail by the river. The joy, oh the joy, of easy movement on fresh powder, listening to happy chickadees, breathing the brisk air, seeing the snow caught in the hollows of the trees and the tufts of white on top of the bushes as we snowshoed miles through the woods.

We might ask ourselves: The things we worry about, are they worth our time and energy? Does distressing about them ever change the outcome? In my experience, the answer is "no." So why give in to being mentally or emotionally jittery? After we make sure our basic needs are being met, we then give those pushy worries a boot out the door.

## *The Best Medicine*

*I'm at that age where the next day my body whispers to me: "Please don't do that again."*

~ Coffee and Jelly Beans cartoon

You've probably heard the saying that "laughter is the best medicine." When the limitations, ambiguities, and fears of elders arrive more quickly each year, having a sense of humor can help enormously. A chuckle or a good-sized laugh proves valuable when we feel pulled into the quicksand of ill-health and weariness, or when we make embarrassing blunders.

I checked the internet and learned that laughter "draws people together in ways that trigger healthy physical and emotional changes in the body." I could have skipped that search. I already knew the results of humor from experience. When we laugh, we forget for a while what worries us. We sense greater ease about life in general. Our spirit feels lighter, less caught in encumbering stuff when we share a joke, a comic strip, or a story about a personal goof that's characteristic of old age.

After my aunt entered her mid-eighties and moved to a senior residence, she chose to be as upbeat and cheerful as possible. One of the ways she achieved this was by sending a cartoon via email to those of us who welcomed their arrival. Aunt Jo also found something to laugh about in the dining room, which was quite easy with misspelled words showing up almost daily on the menu, such as a burger sandwich spelled "buger," sounding a lot like "booger."

There's a difference between making fun of people's blunders and being amused at the foibles of old age. One of the safest ways to make sure we aren't hurting anyone's feelings is to tell stories about our own bloopers. I recall laughing so much my face hurt when I visited my friends Joe and Betty and heard them tell about their attempt earlier that day to drive to a park quite a distance from their home so they could go on a healthy walk. Before they made it there, old age had its say.

Joe and Betty were just a block from home when they heard a thump and a splash outside of the car's back window. When they stopped and got out, they saw Joe's metal coffee mug on the cement. He had inadvertently placed it on the top of the car and forgotten to take it off before driving away. Turning around, they went home to get another cup of coffee. When they entered the house, Betty saw her cell phone that she had forgotten to take along. Off they went again. This time after three minutes they heard another strange sound. Stopping again, they discovered that Joe had placed his billfold and phone on top of the car while he was making sure he had his coffee cup with him. Turning the car around again, this time they searched the street to locate the items. Luckily they spotted the billfold but were unable to retrieve the $20 dollar bill it once held. No phone. After a diligent hunt, they decided to go on, but as they got into the car, Joe noticed that the phone was still on top of the car; it had been there the whole time.

Greatly relieved, they once more set forth. And this time, good news, Betty spotted the twenty dollar bill sitting happily by the side of the street. And so began the trek of this older couple as they went for a walk.

As I drove home after visiting these friends, I felt a clearing space inside myself. The emotional turmoil I'd recently been experiencing with the world's endless pain had crowded out my joy, but with that visit the stress flew away. The laughter that kept slipping into our conversation cleansed my spirit. We can most always find something funny about the never-ending times we misplace or lose things. I'm smiling even now recalling a friend telling how he couldn't find his phone: "My latest Elder Caper. Last remembered place was in my car. Got in, sat in driver's seat, searched to no avail. That night got in again with a flashlight and searched every crevice. No phone. My neighbor came over and found it right away. I had been sitting on the phone in the car while I was looking for it."

Those crazy sorts of things naturally happen to everyone, but they happen more frequently as we age. We can choose to be irritated with ourselves, or chuckle and accept this as part of our increasing lack of concentration. Not long ago I got myself into one of those situations where I could either castigate myself for stupidity or think it rather funny. When I went to pay in the self-serve section of the supermarket, I decided to use a gift card for that store. But no matter how I tried, the card would not complete the purchase. A young clerk who looked about eighteen years old came over to assist me. After the card did not work for him either, he held it up closely to take a look, and with a smirk (as in, "What a stupid old lady") announced that it was the wrong card. And away he went, undoubtedly to hee-haw about it with other employees. Initially, I felt embarrassed, but as I left the store I chose to smile about it on the way home. Choosing to approach what I did as just one of aging's goofs took the sting out of my humiliation.

Quips related to annoying health or memory issues tend to lessen irritation and help us be more accepting of them. Bill refers to his heart doctors as "the electricians." Poet Donald Hall commented about a jest his mother made as her memory slowed down: "She said that one of the advantages of being ninety was that she could read a detective story again, only two weeks after she first read it, without a notion of which character was the villain." Friend Tanya asked if I knew of anyone with her urinary problem—having to rush to the bathroom and barely making it there, even though she did not know she had the urgent need to relieve herself until she parked her car in the garage. Tanya jokingly terms this as *the garage door syndrome*. I haven't had that situation, but I did create a mantra for when I am not yet home from a walk and wishing there was a bathroom nearby. I call it *mind over bladder*.

Some elders find humor in situations more readily than others. Laughter lives in my ancestral genes. My maternal great aunts survived hard times. Some were widowed early with children to raise; all of them were short on money. They would get together, tell jokes, and find all sorts of things to fill the room with hearty laughter. Their joy didn't minimize their problems, but it distracted and led them away from their daily drudgery.

# III

# Gifts of Elderhood

## "Old Tracks"

Looking back on the paths of life taken,
the old tracks reveal well-worn treads,
some washed away by rivers of sorrow
or wind-swept with burdens of busyness.

How many are the footsteps of a long life,
how plentiful the wisdom of vast experience.
How much to be learned from loss and gain,
providing strength enough to set forth anew.

The gifts of a long lifetime settle into place,
some still fresh and many honed long ago,
some ripened and ready for the harvest,
others maturing as the path of age narrows.

The past propels the old into the unfamiliar.
Learn from where the tracks have furrowed

but do not try to remain in the deep grooves.
Be ready to travel farther on the trackless path.

Turn with learned trust toward the open space,
believe there is more than today's revelation.
Keep the mind wide awake, the heart resplendent,
hold out readied gifts while ripening continues.

~ Joyce Rupp

# *Welcoming Our Gifts*

*Now is the time to celebrate and appreciate who we are, who we have become on our life journey.*

~Janet Schaeffler, OP

Before we can welcome the benefits of our elder years, we have to trust that those benefits exist. Florida Scott-Maxwell wrote the following in *The Measure of My Days*, her memoir of experiencing old age: "A man once said to me, 'I don't mind your telling me my faults, they're stale, but don't tell me my virtues. When you tell me what I could be it terrifies me.' I was surprised then, I understand now, because I believe we may be faced by the need of living our strengths." Do we trust that we have our own set of assets?

In *Living Presence*, Kabir Helminski emphasizes the reality of these strengths dwelling in us:

> The well-being, the beauty, and the love we seek outside ourselves are truly within. The paradox is that as we discover what is within, the outer things will increasingly awaken these inner qualities.... What attracts us in the outer world is only putting us in touch with the hidden treasure within us.

Young people gradually come to know and trust in their abilities. Elders need to re-call theirs and also recognize new ones. Plus, we require different gifts to travel the path of the later years. With a slowing of physical agility and mental acuity, our enduring, positive qualities are what allow us to welcome each day with unflappable courage.

Sometimes older persons find it challenging to detect what might be positive about living as long as they have. If our Western culture were more affirming and kinder to its oldest citizens, then being an elder would consist of a stage of life in which we naturally believed in its worth. We cannot help but be influenced by how others view us. "How we age," advises Connie Zweig,

> is a more individual, subjective experience with health outcomes tied as much to beliefs and values as to biology. When we internalize agist messages and believe that becoming old makes us useless, worthless, unattractive, and inferior to youth, when we believe that it means only decline, dementia, suffering, and death, then we behave accordingly.

When we move beyond a detrimental view of ourselves and trust in our significance, then an awareness of the constructive aspects of older age opens up. The gifts of the late years may not become readily visible until we've accepted leaving behind what no longer fits for our present circumstance. The energetic ways we've found to appreciate and express who we are won't work as well, whether those ways have been physical, mental, spiritual, or relational. But there are fresh sources that can give us reasons to rejoice in who we are, and to trust our inner strength to support us in our aging process.

One of the most valuable gifts of older people involves the ability to listen. Showing a genuine interest in how others are faring contributes to their well-being. Who does not appreciate being listened to? Clerks, medical personnel, caregivers, hairdressers, and bus drivers are real people with real lives and real concerns. What a gift we give them, as well as to the people we live with or meet regularly, when we move our attention toward them and away from ourselves. We set aside our concerns and concentrate on someone else. This doesn't mean being snoopy or overly solicitous; rather, it means being sincerely interested in another human being. Elders have a myriad of other gifts but none is quite so precious as being a listening, caring presence.

Another prized gift of Elderhood involves the growing freedom we experience—freedom to be less attached to material items, freedom to go slower and savor the satisfaction coming from previously overlooked kindnesses, freedom to be more in touch with what really counts, more leisure time to enjoy valued relationships, whether these are peer friendships or spending time with grandchildren or other relatives.

Equally freeing is the self-awareness and self-knowledge we acquire that allow us to choose the friends we have and the groups we want to belong to, with fewer reservations or self-doubt. We have a much better sense of what is for our good while at the same time not thinking less of someone else because their interests do not align with ours.

The ability to read is among Elderhood's assets that I personally relish—having the luxury of time to do this for pleasure rather than a professional update, or trying to fit it into a full-time work schedule. Whether this be fiction or non-fiction, I get to decide what resonates as reliable and trustworthy, and know that I can give myself permission to set something aside without any qualms. Not that I plan to be stuck in my own preferences, but rather I have grown to trust what is insightful, challenging, and life-giving.

We allow ourselves to enjoy life for the sake of enjoying life. My artist friend Marian described this well when she spoke about being in her mid-eighties: "What I notice is that I don't feel I 'have to' anymore—schedule programs, take commissions, or make deadlines. But I still would like to continue listening to what is deepest in me, painting from that. It's the 'compulsion' that I've retired from. I'm so grateful for being relieved from my life-long intensity to 'change the world,' to make it a better place by *doing*. Now it's more like we're all in this together—the triune One and each of us creatures—co-creating, healing, nourishing, dreaming."

Celebrating our gifts doesn't mean we have to have all our body-parts oiled and working to their fullest capacity. Nor does it imply having a perfect memory, easy mobility, and spot-free skin. As we become more accepting and in tune with our inner strengths, we look toward the untrod path into our future and know we have much to welcome in our old age. These strengths and beneficial qualities will see us through until we reach the end of the road.

When we celebrate Elderhood, we applaud who we are *now*. We've come so far, traveled to the deeper reaches of our inner being, lived through unbelievable changes on our exterior path of life, and made it to this place where we continue living on a marvelous planet. We have learned so much about the complexities and beauty of our self and others.

What satisfaction we receive as we uncover and claim the gifts of our interior orchard.

# *The Gift of Wisdom*

*Wisdom is the art of living in rhythm with your soul, your life and the divine.*

~ John O'Donohue

On a day when Maxine was taking care of her granddaughter, they were walking outside when a bird flew by. Maxine asked, "Do you know what kind of bird that is?" Three-year-old Kyla paused, furrowed her brow, and then answered, "Gramma, I was just born; I can't know everything." Even those of us born long ago cannot "know everything," but we do have a tremendous amount of insight and understanding gleaned from our many years of life.

Certain authors such as Zalman Schachter-Shalomi refer to elders who've gained wisdom as *sages.* Schachter-Shalomi refers to being a sage as "a process," a way that older adults use "the dormant powers of intuition" to "become seers who feed wisdom back into society." This is the kind of wisdom Irish poet John O'Donohue describes as "a deeper way of knowing," one that comes about with reflection and a growing trust of our interior guidance and insight. Being a sage is not about how much knowledge our intellect contains. It is about the perceptions residing in us and the capacity to access this enriching and meaningful content.

One day when I met with our Elderhood group, I read some passages from Schachter-Shalomi's book, *From Age-ing to Sage-ing*. I asked if they considered themselves to be sages now that they were in their nineties. Without hesitation, each one responded "No." They felt that being a sage was far beyond them, that it involved being some sort of mystical figure, an extremely knowledgeable individual set apart by special abilities. They imagined a sage as someone able to peer into the depths of life with more intensity and lucidity than they could muster. Even though these elders could not envision themselves as sages, I could. These reflective women knew themselves well. They'd lived a lot of years and grown from that "knowing." It's not so much that they continually spouted awe-inspiring statements. Rather, their demeanor and response to life's disparities reflected the peaceful integrity of a sage's authenticity.

If we wonder whether we have accrued wisdom now that we are older, we can look at what we thought and believed when we were twenty or thirty years younger. What has changed in our thinking? Do we treat ourselves and others differently than we did then? What core beliefs now guide us? What is our current approach and response to the uncertainties of our life and those of the world? Are our approach and response different from those in the past? Do they instill peace?

As wisdom grows, certain viewpoints or ideas that used to give meaning to our lives gradually intensify, change significantly, or alter in perspective. At the same time, we may feel as if we intellectually know less than ever, have fewer certitudes about the enigmas of existence. This, too, is wisdom

—recognizing how much cannot be rationally understood or explained. We still seek truth, but we find it lives within us much more than outside of us.

If we are becoming sages, we will keep growing in being open, loving, accepting, and nonjudgmental. Our demands that life has to go our way will soften. We will increase our dedication to the daily process of being transformed in both character and conduct. Genuine wisdom recognizes a communion with self, others, and the larger world, a sense of unity that quiets self-seeking and expands the soul's harmony. In his novel, *Siddhartha,* Herman Hesse precisely sums up this gift when he describes what has come to fruition for his long-questing, now-aged, main character: "Within Siddhartha there slowly grew and ripened the knowledge of what wisdom really was and the goal of his long seeking. It was nothing but a preparation of the soul, a capacity, a secret art of thinking, feeling, and breathing thoughts of unity at every moment of life."

As elders, our life-experience and the wisdom that ensues is certainly greater than in our youth. It's not surprising, then, that we might want to insert our suggestions and sentiments for how others ought to proceed with their lives. Whatever the topic, I've come to the conclusion it's best to keep the verbal door closed. All too often I've wanted to offer counsel, anything from chiding children who fail to visit parents, to challenging older friends who lose their spunk for adventure. I've learned it's best to just listen. My miscalculations and wrong turns have led me to be wiser. Why not give others this same opportunity? Besides, what I envision as good for myself may not be what is best for someone else. I rely on four helpful words: *Keep your mouth shut.* If it's quite apparent someone much younger is wandering into rattlesnake territory and could be helped with a warning, I ask: “Okay if I suggest something?” If the response is “yes,” I offer an opinion—only once. Over and done. No future, squeaky carping about following my “astute advice.”

Unwanted events bring opportunities to grow in wisdom, to take what we experience and learn from it, to integrate the head with the heart, the past with the present. Quiet reflection is one of the most essential and valuable ways to do this. By pondering our exterior and interior life, we gradually gain, in Jungian therapist Helen Luke’s words, “a spirit of discriminating wisdom, separating moment by moment the wheat from the chaff, so that [we] may know in both wheat and chaff their meaning and their value in the pattern of the universe.”

Various kinds of reflection move us inward as we consider pieces of our lives. As we do so, we gain in our aptitude to understand how these fit or do not fit with what we currently believe to have meaning and value. We also develop wisdom by how we tend to the suffering that comes our way. Marilyn McEntyre has noticed, “Though suffering doesn’t necessarily make people wise, it seems that wisdom rarely, if ever, comes without some suffering.”

The wise elder has found a strengthening way to grow through what has been, and may still be, painful and undesired. Our wisdom also arises from joyful experiences, from how we have been affirmed and loved, and other myriad moments of gladness visiting us. We acknowledge the right and basic need of every individual to access this gladness.

What a precious gift, this wisdom dwelling in us. As we pause, reflect, and gather the remnants of life, they gradually form a more meaningful rhythm in our aged existence.

# *The Blessing of Be-ing*

*Just to be is a blessing. Just to live is holy.*

~ Abraham Joshua Heschel

A friend of mine has an outgoing personality. She thrives on relationships and action. I'm most at home with long stretches of quiet and less scurrying around. Does my friend value reflective time and quiet? Absolutely. Do I value relationships and social activity? Unquestionably. What most brings our spirits energy and joy comes from different sources. "One size fits all" doesn't work for anyone and surely not for elders. In this regard, however, we do all need certain amounts of both *doing and being.*

I'm writing about this because our Western culture still places more value and emphasis on the action or *doing* aspect. We've been programmed from early on to get going, be productive, "make a living," use the juice of life in every way possible. This compulsion is tightly woven into our society's genes. When we move into old age, no matter how hard we try, we aren't going to be able to produce all that vitality. We simply have much less of it.

What is the consolation of our limbs moving more slowly, needing more rest, enjoying "doing nothing"? Our spirit cries out for this deceleration of activity. Our body insists on moving us in that direction. We can fight this change of *doing* less and *being* more or welcome it as a natural and positive development, one that allows us the opportunity and presence to ripen the qualities dwelling within the essence of who we truly are. This is one of the valuable consolations of slowing down.

When I was in my forties, the introverted part of me discovered and resonated with the quote from Rabbi Heschel that introduces this reflection. His words gave me permission to trust my longing for less action. I began feeling the freedom to reduce my pressured activity and quiet the inner voice that said I had to show something of value for everything I did. I've had that quote hanging in my living room ever since. What I did not learn until several decades later is that Heschel's statement was part of a talk given to older people. Now I understand more clearly its inherent truth: *our lives have value in and of themselves.* We do not have to be caught up in action all the time in order to respect ourselves and others. Each moment is holy, sacred, and worthwhile in itself. No need to prove anything, to anyone.

So much resides within the fabric of who we truly are. Be-ing allows us space to move inward, to look more closely at what stirs inside of us. Going slower enables us to quiet ourselves enough to observe our thoughts, witness our feelings, sort through our beliefs; to glean what they tell us about who we are and how we are to engage with our final years. When we roam around inside ourselves we listen to questions previously ignored: What asks for our understanding? What cries out to be set free? What longs to be assured of value and acceptance? What whispers to us of hope or concern for a future generation?

When we are older we can and ought to continue to be active, but the focus moves from activity as dominant or obligatory to relaxation and less insistence on getting things done, from living on the external surface of life to spending time exploring its depths and enjoying the hidden realms that we've missed, where so much enrichment resides. No more hurrying, pushing, and plunging ourselves into activity and responsibility. No more striving. No more "you gotta," and "you oughta" when it comes to choosing how we move through our days.

It's time to cease identifying ourselves by what we do. We are no longer persons known mainly by our profession or past achievements. We are who we are. Will we trust that "just to be is a blessing?" That our life as we live it each day is holy?

"When you have all the time in the world," writes Robin Wall Kimmerer, "you can spend it, not on going somewhere, but on being where you are. So I stretch out, close my eyes, and listen to the rain."

One of the best examples of an elder who knows how to do this is a dear Canadian friend. Several years ago, he sent the following reflection:

*Eighty-five Years Old Today*

> I am 85. Healthy and happy, alive and well. I love and am loved. Lucky I am and blessed beyond my wildest dreams. Today I celebrate a special time in my life beyond anything I could have expected. Have accepted my commitment to love all whom I come in contact with: friends, people on the street, and subway travelers, especially those who offer me their seat.

I have morphed—evolved—into a friendly old guy who enjoys chatting up people, who feels he offers a bit of good will, when he says "Good morning" to strangers on the street.

No longer want to change the world, be famous or rich. Have not however relinquished my quest for a noble deed. However, I've learned how to do nothing and brag that I am very good at it. Even though it's still not easy to tolerate the boredom of sitting on the couch staring at the wall, or lying awake in the middle of the night. But that is part of the territory.

Hey, I've lived my life. And yet I sense that there is something more. For I would leave nothing unlived or unsaid. I would drink deeply from the cup of my humanity. Life is good.

Blessings and love,

Austin

Doesn't that sound like my friend has taken to heart the very essence of what Abraham Joshua Heschel encouraged? It's great that Austin is not dismayed by what he terms "boredom." He doesn't try, as Kathleen Dowling Singh warns, to go "looking for distractions, escapes, from loneliness and boredom, the two lions at the gate of our oldest years." Austin chooses to enter life at his own speed and with his own loving heart. We are meant to do the same.

# *Mentors of Aging*

*A mentor is someone who allows you to see the hope inside yourself.*

~ Oprah Winfrey

If questions beset us with the onset of older age, wondering how to engage positively with this stage of life, we can find direction and courage from people who served as mentors of aging for us. Remembering what drew us to them and how they approached their last decades inspires us to maintain fortitude, retain constructive outlooks, and keep interested in life beyond our narrow sphere. These mentors may not have been people we knew personally. We may have become acquainted with them through their memoirs or marveled at what we learned in other ways about how these older persons lived an admirable and inviting life. Depending on how we participate in our aging years, we, too, evolve as mentors for those who live on after we are gone.

Mentors of aging influence others not so much by what they say as by their presence and how they engage in the ripening process. Ideally, this includes a continued openness to learning and growing, a willingness to experience life in its abundance, humbly accepting what can no longer be expected or changed, and exuding an abiding peacefulness.

We receive a translucent, lovely welcome when we are in the presence of aging mentors. These wise guides are at home with themselves. They do not deny their limitations or the adverse advancements of body and mind. Instead, they choose to not focus on them. Mentors of aging convey a persistent love of life, interior attentiveness to what stirs and asks to be known, and a noticeable lack of speaking often about medical tribulations.

We like being with these people. Their very personhood gives us hope that we, too, can make this journey of getting old with confidence. More than anything, perhaps, is the sense that they are reaching the finishing line with transforming love oozing from the pores of their spirit. Their love silently slides into us like gentle waves washing upon the shore of a serene lake.

When I consider some of the mentors of aging who inspired me because of how they entered into their final years, I think first of my mother. Constant back pain thwarted her walking ability, she had low energy as a result of COPD and diabetes—yet these physical woes did not stop her from enjoying life. What I remember vividly are my mother's strong hugs in greeting and farewell, an ability to win at Scrabble (she rarely lost), a delight in meeting new people, and the intimate conversations we had about such things as her future death and the funeral plans she was making. She shared these with me as matter-of-fact information. I hope I can face life and death with such acceptance and fearlessness. I want to live with as much verve as my mother did, no matter how severe my physical impairments might be.

Some mentors have inspired me to continue to expand my knowledge. Sister Evangelista Griffin loved to learn. Even as she celebrated her hundredth birthday, she had a stack of library books that she was reading and studying. In her mid-eighties Pat Sloan Skinner continued to introduce me to her favorite authors, especially to new poets she had discovered. She would read their poems to me with a smile in her voice. Cousin Dorothy and her husband Ed Schnoes eased their way into Elderhood with the most gentle graciousness and joy. Just to be around them was like breathing fresh air. When I would leave after a visit with them in their home, and later in a Care Center where widowed Dorothy lived, I would have less debris in my mind and heart. They didn't have to say astute things. The unencumbered way they chose to live, their peace with how they were aging—this was their mentoring. I always felt a spaciousness of heart after being in their presence.

It was well worth the hour's drive to spend time with Bernice Donovan. She was in her late nineties the day I walked into her home and found she had a kettle of her homemade soup on the stove and a pot of tea brewing. Even when Bernice became bedridden a year or so later, she greeted me with the glee of receiving someone who had been away for forty years. Bernice never failed to be interested in events around the globe, and our conversations were spiced with her latest findings from delving into world news and developments.

Ida Delperdang remains one of my favorite inspirations of how to age. I cannot recall this great aunt ever talking about how old she was or the unwanted consequences of being in a nursing home. She seemed to be at peace wherever she lived, remaining humble and unassuming until her death. How I relished her crackly voiced "Hi" and her robust laughter when she told a joke. I so want to have a spirit like this dear woman's.

Ever since I was a small child I was touched by my uncle's kind and gentle manner. Bob farmed not far from us, so I saw him often. He could be a tease but never once did I hear him discount or verbally disparage anyone. I felt he accepted each one in my family with non-judgment. As Uncle Bob aged, his qualities of kindness and acceptance mellowed even more. When I'm having a less than contented day, remembrance of this uncle's kindheartedness helps to keep my impatient irritability and grouchiness at bay.

The insights and encouragement about aging that I've received from other elders includes what I have learned by observing successful men and women move graciously away from accolades and professional achievements. Other mentors have taught me that it's possible to have poor health and still keep a positive outlook. When I witness poets and authors continuing to create in their Elderhood years, they lend me hope that I, too, might continue to draw forth and share my talents as an older writer.

While few of us have all the characteristics of mentoring, we each have some of them, enough to affect and influence forthcoming elders in their choices and decisions. If those of us now in late life develop the gifts we possess—the ability to be mentors of inspiration, fortitude, kindness, and hope—then the next generation will be ready to find their way to old age in a healthy and enjoyable manner when they arrive at this ripened stage.

It's not that we deliberately aim to be an example or inspiration, not that we must speak in wise and eloquent terms about our condition in life. Rather, we decide day by day to live our life as well as we can, to be of genuine good cheer, and to give others our fullest, most-heartfelt consideration.

# IV

# Loss

## "Search for What Is Left"

Perhaps only a tiny whisper
    in the heart,
a word of compassion to carry
    the desolate
through storms that bash and batter
    the ill, grieved, broken,
    and wearied.

Perhaps only a thimbleful
    of thin hope
when dreams of what might
    have been
are dashed to pieces on the
    stiff rocks
of old age and its increasing
    infirmities.

Perhaps only a heartbeat of
    quiet love pulses
after those counted as precious
    depart at death's arrival,
    a withering
    of the heart's happiness.

Look for quiet consolation
    in what remains;
welcome the hope that persists
    in thriving.
Count on a steady portion of inner
    strength.
Step beyond loss and search for
    what is left.

~ Joyce Rupp

# *Inevitable Loss*

> *There is hardly any limit to the ways loss will find us, entering into our lives not only through the death of someone we love but also through the myriad other ways life can wrest from us what we hold dear.*
>
> ~ Jan Richardson

In youth, we gather. In old age, we give away. Our valued physical and material assets dissipate steadily the longer we live. What is taken from us or what we reluctantly dispose of slips away. By the time we are eighty and beyond, one might think we would be accustomed to this. But we never get used to it. Instead, we gradually adjust to inevitable loss thrusting its way into our life.

My friend Tanya knows about depletion. She broke her femur, spent over a month in a rehabilitation facility, moved from that place at her children's insistence to a senior residence for assisted living in the heart of the city. (Assisted living = insisted living.) This led to her selling her beautiful home in the woods. The final blow was being informed she could no longer have a driver's license. These accumulated changes came about in less than six months. No wonder Tanya felt crushed by the sudden and large amount of transition demanded of her.

Not all loss is this distressful for older people. Sometimes necessary changes can bring about good results. For example, when her failing health necessitated her moving into a nursing home, my aunt, who had always been an extrovert, found that she enjoyed living there, surrounded by people who eased her loneliness. In another case, a widow felt relieved and lost her fear of living alone by moving into a senior residence. And a man who turned in his driver's license admitted his growing concern that he might have caused serious injury to another driver because of his limited eyesight. Then there was the letter I received from a stranger elated that her husband had finally died—"putting an end to years of his demoralizing verbal abuse"—and the older nun with persistent bodily pain who stood by the coffin of a community member and whispered, "Lucky her."

Many of the losses that seep into Elderhood are undesired. They drain energy and shrink options for finding a cessation from these depletions. Whether physical, intellectual, spiritual, or relational, forfeiture of what has given meaning and blessing to our lives challenges us to adjust. When more of what we have appreciated departs, it's like comfy clothes that no longer fit after we've lost a lot of weight. Try as we might, we cannot wear them anymore. Accepting the unavoidable—this summons us to have daily openness toward change. When I met a stranger at an eightieth birthday party, we spoke about entering this phase of life. She described how she walked through her home one day looking at all the lovely items she had collected through the years, saying to herself, "I can't. I won't let go of any of these things." I smiled and said nothing but thought, "Oh, yes, you will, one way or another. Time and age will bend your control and force you to either give them away or have them wrested from you." My hope is that she, and all of us, can come to accept that material treasures are not what will give our souls lasting peace.

In the Bible, Abraham is acclaimed for leaving his homeland at age seventy-five (Genesis 12:1–9). That was a brave thing to do, but we who are of a similar age or older notice that this is about the only part of the story that relates to ours. Abraham "took *all* his possessions with him," while we downsize, downsize, downsize, so we can squeeze into the ever smaller spaces that become our home. Likewise, Abraham was told he would be the father "of a great nation." He had big things ahead of him, certainty of success and assurance of productivity, while we lose the ability or incentive to be industrious and are no longer able to claim noted achievements in what we do.

Where I find courage and inspiration from this story is in the risk Abraham and his wife Sarah exhibited by moving into the unknown and adjusting to uncertainty. They left a secure situation and had to trust that something good lay ahead for them, and it did. I trust this for myself, for all of us who courageously move onward and embrace the indefinite territory of the future.

Even though losses are unavoidable with older age, elders do not have to cede all their pleasures or lie down in defeat. In *God Never Blinks*, Regina Brett reminds her readers:

> There's an old saying people use to cope through bad times. This too shall pass. Most people don't want to use that when it comes to the good times. We don't want them to pass. We want them to last forever. But sooner or later, everything changes.

> The secret is to ride life like a raft in a river and let it carry you through the white water and the still water and beyond. Float on down like a leaf, holding on to nothing, trusting the flow of the river.

That's easier said than done when pain intensifies and physical and mental abilities shrink, when there is less in life within our range of control. Who could blame anyone for feeling depressed or dismal after receiving a medical report that one's health will continue to worsen? Who would try to convince someone that better days are ahead when a sustaining companionship of fifty-five years slips away through death? Who has the audacity to offer cheerful slogans of "things will get better" to people who have been scammed out of their financial savings? We aren't immune to feeling sad, lonely, bereft, or depressed because of our losses, but we can refuse to allow them to strangle our peace.

Brett's image is helpful as an emotional and mental response to unwanted loss. Picturing ourselves on the river of life where the flow of divine presence carries us along with tender compassion can sustain our resilience. The older we grow, the more we turn to this image of supportive confidence, the more likely we will be assured that loss is a natural part of the aging journey and that it need not destroy our spirit.

We know we are growing old. We know we will have more depletions. It is our attitude toward them that either instills peace or creates a troublesome angst.

# *The Depleting Pond*

*Every loss we experience in our lifetime*
*has the capacity to deepen us,*
*to widen the channel of soul life flowing into us.*

~ Francis Weller

Jane Kenyon creates a poignant metaphor in "The Nursing Home." This is a powerful poem about the effects of aging at the end of life, specifically about her aging mother who resided in a care center. Kenyon compares the experience of her parent to that of a horse grazing on a hillside where someone comes every night and pulls the fences of the pasture in closer and closer. Gradually the horse stops running "wide loops" and "tight circles" and simply feeds on dusty grass. In the last line, Kenyon concludes this image of a steady demise by requesting that the "Master" come and place a "light halter" on the horse to bring her home.

A parallel image came to me one day as I paused by a pond near Blue Heron Lake. I stopped to watch a heron standing ankle-deep in water that was once over a foot deep. The waters that filled the area had continued to contract from the grassy shore. The place was slowly dying due to the severe drought of past summers. I thought, "The pond is shrinking—just like my aging life is slowly closing in on me—and there's little I can do about it."

A few weeks later, a large flock of mallard ducks flew in on their migration route and settled on that same depleting pond. Soon they had their heads under water and butts in the air, foraging for food. Because of the lower water level, the ducks could easily reach the tasty treats of nutritious string algae. "So, too," I mused, "with age I develop interior assets to be enjoyed and shared with others even though my energy and physical abilities are receding."

We may find it difficult to retain a belief that something positive will be released within us as the consequence of a dwindling aspect of our self. I wonder if the slow-paced man who walked around another pond years ago when I was in my forties knew about one of those hidden gifts that he was able to give me. On that day I trudged along with downcast face and heart, ruminating about a painful situation that ripped joy away from my spirit. When I met him on the path, he looked my way and advised, "Oh, cheer up. It can't be as bad as all that." At first, I felt irritated by his remark, but as I walked on farther I recognized the wisdom in it. I had let a painful situation drain my gladness. The hurt wasn't worth allowing confident energy to slip away from me. Like the ducks foraging for food in the depleting pond, the aging stranger provided the nutrient of wisdom for what I needed that day. I felt better and began to heal.

Changes in physical health certainly illustrate the effects of depletion. Yesterday I used the word "maintain one's health" when talking about "getting older" with friends now in their mid-nineties. John amended my comment with "No, at our age, it's not *maintaining*. It's about how to slow the *reduction*." He was speaking from his present experience of losing an ability to walk only a short distance. I could hear the combination of frustration and the reluctant surrender in his voice.

When I interviewed Anne, she described health problems that had recently emptied both her husband and herself of a great deal of vitality. She went on to say, "What gives me real happiness and satisfaction is the love and interaction with my children and grandchildren." I know that Anne also continues to serve as a spiritual guide for the women in her church. A decrease of her former energy has not daunted Anne's efforts to nurture others' growth. If anything, the decrease has reinforced a desire to share her expertise in spite of depletion.

Our losses often sneak up on us gradually. Like bodies that slowly weaken and limbs that progressively wear out, friendships once strong and enduring can become more like wilted lettuce, not very nourishing or enthusing due to the strain of passing years. Each of us may have changed in ways that weakened a once-strong connection. We can choose to try to revive these relationships or let them slowly slip away through little or no contact. We need not chide ourselves about this. Rather, we can see it as another of life's inevitable forfeitures that we do not invite but that happen, nevertheless. We can be grateful for what we gave and received when the friendship flourished; and we can let it dissolve when appropriate to do so.

Alice Camille, a religious educator, acknowledges the fences being drawn in for herself, the water in her pond of life shrinking.

> Many of my companions—and I myself—are past full bloom now. Presently we're on a new quest: to make peace with our diminishment. It was glorious

> to be young, we confess to each other. Yet there's glory in maturity too, even with its losses, aches, and debility. Diminishment is a quieter process than the unfurling of youth, or the display of midlife capability. Later life is about releasing instead of acquiring, growing lighter rather than gathering gravity.

I've had brief moments of clarity about being readied to wear that lightness, the continual shedding of what once provided security and stability. One understanding of this came at age seventy-five when I moved from a reclusive cottage in the woods to an apartment in a bustling neighborhood. I dreaded leaving that lovely solitude of twenty years. Plus, the apartment was exceedingly small compared to the cottage. When I saw the sparse cupboard space in its kitchen I thought I wouldn't be able to manage, but manage I have. After a while I adjusted to the lack of space, and now I do not mind it. I truly enjoy where I live with the voices of children nearby and a vast eastern horizon filled with sunrises and sightings of full moons—something I never had at the cottage with trees sheltering it from the sky.

My residential move confirmed for me how options will keep shrinking, whether they're about material things, bodily health, social relationships, or other areas of life. Like Jane Kenyon's corralled horse, the parameters of how much time we have here on Earth and how freely we can live upon it will keep closing in with the unfolding years.

Fortunately, aging also gifts us with the option of a continual enlargement in the space of our hearts. There the fences need not be drawn in. There the nourishment can increase and stay eternally fresh. In the heart's space, there is always room for expanding love.

# *The Crowd Grows Bigger*

*I am ninety-one years old.*
*Not many people I once knew are still alive.*

~ Christina Baker Kline

As we age, our losses accumulate and affect more of our inner strongholds. This is especially so when the people who filled our life with natural compatibility, supportive care, easy laughter, and comforting kinship keep dying. With their absence, there's one less person to chat with, to join in attending social functions, to reminisce with about "the good times" and raise concerns about the mess our world is in.

Yesterday I sent a note of sympathy to a woman whose last remaining sibling had died of a heart attack. I felt compassion for her, knowing that she was experiencing the unique pang of grief that sets in when there's no one else left in the family of origin except oneself. For anyone in the later decades, it's tough to continually bid farewell to the parade of relatives and friends who go on their way. I never comprehended what my mother meant when she would say, "All my friends are gone." I'd think, "Well, but you have us—your children and grandchildren." I didn't get what it was like for her to not have peers who understood her experiences and history in a way we never could.

Another part of Elderhood involves old friends, especially those who live far away. When we get in touch or see each other, we have no way of knowing whether that will be the last time. After visiting a beloved friend who lives three hundred and fifty miles away and saying goodbye at the door of her apartment, the only solace I had at the time was a line from Kate DiCamillo's novel, *Flora and Ulysses*: "So we said goodbye to each other the best way we could. We said: '*I promise to always turn back toward you.*'" That thought comforted me, as did my friend's text message the next day:

> These goodbyes are tender in the elder years—knowing full well the reality of it. We may not see one another again. The strong hug, the tender gaze of friendship in one another's eyes, a decision to trust love's strength to last far beyond physical presence. These goodbyes could end in tears; instead, a warm river of gratitude flows through the perhaps-last-farewell, realizing how enriched, how favored is the beauty of an enduring relationship.

We cannot continually be awash in grief as more people we care about die, even though their departure saddens us. I remember my mother's phone call telling me that one of her life-long friends had died. Mom's voice sounded calm. I couldn't detect sadness. Just matter-of-fact news. Now I understand. You cannot allow every death to drown you in grief at this stage of life or you'll never swim to the surface again. You recognize the loss for what it is. You accept it. You are grateful. Then you go on. There is nothing else to do but go forward. Live as best you can.

This ache of losing peers came through in an email from an eighty-three-year-old relative who made it through the deaths of her husband and two children. I thought perhaps she would not feel so deeply about a future loss, but no, there it was again. She wrote:

> Well, I'm going through losing my best friend. She died Tuesday. Her death hit me harder than I expected. Brought forth all the deaths in the last eight years, plus the past two months. I have been blessed with many close friends but have sure lost a lot. I was feeling mopey about it when an old friend called. We used to talk every morning for years but then changes came into her life that prevented us from having the conversations. She called to see if we could get together on Tuesday. I see God's hand in that call.

What a valuable insight for my relative at the very time her heart was again broken open. How do we cope as the crowd of those who leave us increases in number? As with other challenging changes that come with aging, much depends on how we choose to view or approach this continually emptying process. Well-known spirituality author Henri Nouwen provided a framework for my own approach when he noted that the more we love and allow ourselves to suffer because of that love, the more we'll be able to let our hearts grow wider and deeper. In *The Inner Voice of Love*, Nouwen offers a tender consolation about the suffering that comes with the departure of those dear to us:

> When your love is truly giving and receiving, those whom you love will not leave your heart even when

> they depart from you. . . . Yes, as you love deeply the ground of your heart will be broken more and more, but you will rejoice in the abundance of the fruit it will bear. . . . They will become part of your self and thus gradually build a community within you.

The notion of the crowd of departed relatives and friends forming a community within myself is comforting. In fact, there are mornings in my meditation time when I mentally gather around me some of these beloved persons. I invite them to keep me company while I pray. I envision their spirits encircling my being. I draw strength from their abiding love when I'm in the middle of that "crowd." A year ago I wrote in my journal:

> With each death of a dear person, I used to think of my heart as more empty, increasingly hollowed out. But today I know this not to be so. Love remains present, remains in my heart each time there is a farewell. Those who depart simply transition to another realm. My heart does not become a vacant container as the gathering of those who leave grows larger. Instead, my heart is becoming a chalice overflowing with love because each precious one who departs leaves a portion of their love with me.

While we do not cling to those who've departed, we are also deliberate about keeping alive the love-connection between us. We learn to trust as does Anne Rivers Siddons' character, Buddy: "You don't have to be afraid of leaving people and places. You take them with you somewhere inside you."

# *Tabernacles of Absence*

*Out of loneliness*
*Arises the self we never knew.*

~ Nancy Wood

The loneliness inside a friend who was widowed a year earlier reached over and touched my heart as we attended a funeral luncheon. Sitting next to him I observed and felt his exceptional quietness, the pervasive sadness in his eyes as he focused on the food in front of him. I hurt for his loss and wished I could lessen the feeling of absence that permeated his spirit now that he was without his wife of forty-nine years.

The hollow ache that surfaces from inside our spirit originates from various sources, such as lack of a spouse or peers, a longing to reunite with those who have died, a sadness at what can no longer be possible, or the unnamable lonesomeness of Elderhood that is felt keenly in spite of life offering sufficient relationships and relatively good health. The silent reality of approaching death can also stir loneliness underneath the surface of activity when thinking about the beloved people one's death will affect.

Absence and isolation accompany a lot of older people. Because they have fewer living peers among friends and family, this results in spending more time by themselves and having less opportunity for communing with someone who journeyed with them for a good portion of their lives. A certain reluctance to reach out begins to take over, along with a sigh of resignation and an increasing seclusion.

I recall seeing an older man in the post office, just the two of us standing in line a few feet of Covid-distance apart. When I smiled at him as he entered, I detected what I presumed to be the characteristic facial sadness and drooping body of loneliness. I would have preferred just waiting quietly for the postal clerk to return from the back room, but something inside urged me to speak. So I entered into an easy conversation with him for three or four minutes. After the postal clerk stamped my package, I turned to leave, passing by the man who said, "Thanks for being so friendly to me." What a confirmation those words gave to my intuition about his need to be invited to chat. It confirmed my belief that it only takes a brief encounter of kindness to lessen the loneliness of old age.

Singer John Prine's song "Hello in There" addresses this issue directly. It's a moving song posted on a *YouTube* video. As Prine sings of older people's experience of being ignored or forgotten, the faces of elders appear on the screen, each one revealing a certain isolation due to their age and society's indifference to them. John Prine wrote that song at age twenty-two for the older generation. He had learned respect for them when he helped a friend deliver newspapers room to room in a senior care center. Prine's refrain indicates how a brief interlude can soften loneliness:

> You know that old trees just grow stronger
> And old rivers grow wilder every day

Old people just grow lonesome
Waiting for someone to say,
"Hello in there, hello."

The absence felt by elders is not just about relationships with others. My own loneliness comes from a lack of union with an unseen sphere of existence beyond this one. I "know" in an unproven way that there's a tiny thread inside of me, like the thin, silky filament in a spider's web, connecting me to a world beyond this life.

I'm lonely, not for a person but a dimension, a sphere where I know with all my heart true peace and unity exists, no judgment, hatred, indifference. Nothing that divides the union among beings. I believe I knew this once, experienced the utter joy of it. This memory lives in me. This is where I belong. Death will release me, free me, to rejoin that amazing sphere.

Trusting Enduring Love as the maker and guardian of this thread comforts me as I draw closer to the end of my life, but it does not take away the feeling of disconnection. In *Walking with Wonder*, John O'Donohue reflects on how older people "seem to accumulate more and more absences." He then reminds his readers that loneliness affects more than those in late life: "But any life that is vigorous and open to challenge and compassion and the real activity of thought knows that, as we journey, we create many tabernacles of absence within us."

We older persons are not the only ones who suffer the ache of incompleteness. From time to time, loneliness can be located everywhere, in anyone. This inner response to what we long for and miss has become a kind of malady affecting persons of every age. Knowing that this ache goes on in the spirit of countless individuals can serve to lessen our feeling that loneliness is something only those of us growing older experience. It dismisses the notion that if we try hard enough we can ditch loneliness from our existence.

"Have I endured loneliness with grace?" questions Mary Oliver in her poem, "A Thousand Mornings." That "grace" might be to not blame or nag ourselves if we feel lonely, rather, to accept this ache when we experience it. At the same time, we do not sink into the depths of emptiness and lack of connection. Instead, we remember and draw strength from the comforting word "tabernacle" that John O'Donohue uses in referring to loneliness.

A tabernacle is a hollow space intended to hold something sacred. If we are "tabernacles of absence," then our inner sphere of emptiness is a sacred space. We turn to this holy realm within us when loneliness makes itself present. We open ourselves to receive comfort when we trust that a Spirit of Love dwells within our personal tabernacle, the sphere of our heart.

V

# Grief and Healing

## "Sixteen Years"

I thought grief had lost its clammy grip,
that sorrow had finally decided to recede,
but here I am again, regretfully surprised
and saddened, the intensity of the loss
pounding on the door, pleading with me
to be heard, persistently reaching
into what I presumed to be solid joy.

I cannot outrun this determined visitor.
Thorny night dreams slip in too strongly
to leave me alone. What does this grief
want of me now? How much more rigid
sadness? How much more reminding
of what was cherished and lost forever?

Sixteen years since instant departure—
remembering the wise soul-companion

arriving unexpectedly, and staying.
Twenty years of growing into freedom,
twenty years of convincing me to trust
in my worthiness, twenty years of learning
how to be compassionate and merciful.

So now, when grief slides into the night
and intrudes on what has been locked,
I receive her entrance like an evening star,
illuminating the memory of abiding love
in the tender regions of my emptied heart.

~ Joyce Rupp

# *The Need to Lament*

*I pour out my complaint*

~ Psalm 142:2

Suffering and its accompanying grief can barge its way into life at any age and in any form. "I no longer define grief simply as a response to tragedy," explains Tish Harrison Warren. "Grief is commonplace. All of us walk in grief every day, in one way or another. We bear pain and loss, small disappointments and agonizing memories." There is little doubt that grief abounds in Elderhood.

This stage of life naturally brings more reasons to grieve. We've lived longer, so more farewells empty us of significant relationships, our limbs ache, and our brains tend to work less effectively, plus we have more time to reflect on what feels dissonant in society. There is much to lament in the final years. Widowers lose the intimacy and pleasurable times they had with their spouses. Elders with chronic physical pain are forced to limit certain activities. Residents in assisted living move away from satisfying years in their own homes. Older persons no longer allowed to drive remember how they could travel when they wanted and where they chose to go.

One day it occurred to me that our grief over losses is like a steel brush with harsh spikes, painfully scraping away what we no longer are allowed to keep. Grief discloses what is beneath the layers of our lives, reveals the taken-for-granted and purifies us from the rust and grime of daily interactions—pursuits that distract from our innermost essence of love. It opens us to see more clearly who and what is of utmost importance to us.

As we grow older, we meet unwanted circumstances and goodbyes painful enough to split open our hearts and dump loads of sadness into them. Connie Zweig reminds us to be willing to be with the emotional distress resulting from these situations:

> With aging, a key part of emotional repair is learning how to live with our grief. . . . If grieving does not happen consciously, if we don't turn to face our lost loved ones, unmade choices, and unopened invitations, then our sorrows remain hidden in the shadow. Their meanings remain secret, and we are blind to the full range of human life, unable to ripen into adulthood.

Grief prompts us to cry out in sorrow at what we have lost, to name what hurts. This lamenting moves us toward healing and less emotional distress. The Bible's Book of Lamentations describes the destruction and despondency of Jerusalem, a city caught "in the days of her affliction and wandering. All the precious things that were hers in the days of old" (Lamentations 1:7). The city is forsaken because of what is no more. This biblical book of four chapters spills over with sorrowful words—"desolate, lonely, bitterly in the night with tears on her cheeks, no one to comfort her, exile, no resting place, distress, groans, without strength, affliction, sorrow, sapping my strength."

After two chapters of complaint, moaning, and crying out, halfway into the third chapter a glimmer of hope and relief arises: "The steadfast love of the Lord never ceases, his mercies never come to an end, they are new every morning; great is your faithfulness. 'The Lord is my portion,' says my soul, 'Therefore I will hope in him.'" (vv. 22–24) But then it's back to lamenting and venting until the conclusion of chapter 4. This is so like the process of grief with its twists and turns, in and out of sadness, and the brief respites of relief that gradually expand.

When Florida Scott Maxwell writes about her experience of older age, she, too, acknowledges lamentation:

> Perhaps the forms of life that are passing should be mourned, and this may be the right role of age. Perhaps our wail should be part of the paean of life that is being lived. I do not mourn for lost happiness. I do not mourn for myself. I mourn that life is so incomprehensible, and I mourn for this confused age. We old are the wailers. I hear us everywhere."

I can't say that I'm comfortable being a wailer, but I most certainly believe in the value of naming honestly how I feel about what causes sorrow and leads to a reason for lamentation.

When we are grieving there is a difference between acknowledging what has been ripped away from us and whining or complaining. Whining and complaining come about when the person who hurts clutches the distress so tightly it becomes the only focus of thought and conversation. Everyone ought to tend to their miseries, to address what hurts and aches in the body and spirit. Having someone else listen and really hear about our painful experiences assists in bringing about relief. However, after months (and maybe years) of continually regurgitating the same laments, the time comes to emphasize something more positive in one's life, even if this seems to be trivial or provides minimal satisfaction.

In early adulthood I came across Rainier Maria Rilke's *Letters to a Young Poet*. Only in my later years do I see how much his wisdom directed me to tend my sorrows that began with the sudden death of my younger brother when I was twenty-five. In one of his letters, Rilke advises the young poet to pay attention to his sadness.

> Like illnesses that are treated superficially, they only recede for a while and then break out more severely. Untreated they gather strength inside us and become the rejected, lost, and unlived life that we may die of. If only we could see a little farther than our knowledge reaches and a little beyond the borders of our intuition, we might perhaps bear our sorrows more trustingly than we do our joys. For they are the moments when something new enters us, something unknown.

This "something new" comes as we grieve. Rough edges become smooth, old hurts fade, regrets take their leave, and sorrows melt into memories of enduring love.

# *Self-Compassion*

*Many of us know the feeling of having abandoned some part of ourselves as we've journeyed though life.*

~ Jane Prétat

When I was quite young I was admonished with "stop feeling sorry for yourself" if I pouted or let my tears flow too long while experiencing hurt, disappointment, or rejection. As a result, when I grew into adulthood I held onto the false belief that if I paid attention to what troubled me, I was wallowing in too much self-concern. Christopher Germer suggests that if we "cultivate a new relationship to ourselves" regarding our emotional hurts, this will greatly aid healing from them: Germer then offers a way to do this in *The Mindful Path to Self-Compassion*:

> When we're caught up in our pain, we go to war against *ourselves*. . . . Instead of greeting difficult emotions by fighting hard against them, we can bear witness to our own pain and respond with kindness and understanding. That's self-compassion—taking care of ourselves just as we'd treat someone we love dearly . . .

I gradually learned that there's a difference between self-pity and self-compassion. When we pity our self, we sink into our distress, compare our hurt to that of others, lash out at pain-free persons, and become consumed with our inner or outer injuries. With self-compassion, we acknowledge what wounds and grieves us, doing so with the approach of a tender parent embracing a hurting child. We pay attention to what feels wounded and we acknowledge how difficult it is to bear, without over-indulging in what distresses us.

Self-compassion does not nurse a grudge, constantly resent being ill, refuse to forgive, or get immobilized by discouragement. Instead, self-compassion tends to the woundedness and helps it heal by deliberate care and patient understanding. With healthy attentiveness, self-compassion helps us to gather our resilience and move forward, choosing to lovingly care for our hurts while also avoiding giving them excessive attention.

Whether we call on our inner wisdom and resilience, another trusted human being, the Great Comforter, or some other assistance, with self-compassion we give ourself kindness to go through the struggle. Jesus in the Garden of Gethsemane exemplifies this when desperately in need of strength to enter the suffering that awaited him. He had compassion on his loneliness and fear by asking those he mentored to be by his side, to support him as he wrestled in finding strength to face the terror he felt (Luke 22:39–46).

There is a tendency for our deficiencies to glare at us as we grow older. "I come up against my own limitations as against granite," bemoaned Florida Scott-Maxwell. When we feel cranky and out of sorts, we tend to not like ourselves (or anyone else). When we exhibit impatience or make sharp retorts, we consider our spiritual growth in ruins. We can quickly fall into deciding "I'm not a nice person," or "I'm a failure at trying to live virtuously." We blame ourselves for our loneliness when it rises up to choke our joy. We become angry at ourselves or call ourselves "stupid" when misplacing an item or being unable to quickly retrieve a word from our memory. When we are unable to perform some tasks done quickly in the past or we tire more easily, we describe ourselves as "useless" or "lazy." All these situations, and more, call out for self-compassion. If we are to age peacefully, we must cease our reproachful name-calling of ourselves.

Recently I decided to make a cup of tea, poured some water into the electric tea kettle, turned it on, and went back to my office to spend time at the computer. An hour later I realized I'd not returned to the kitchen and made the tea. That was the moment when I could either accept what happened or berate myself with "what a distracted dummy I am." I chose compassion and ignored the negative voice yelling at me. As I made the tea, I smiled, recalling twenty years earlier when I burned out two—yes, two—tea kettles on the stove in one year. Did I worry then about age affecting my memory and ability to stay focused? No (although I *did* chide myself for being absent-minded). So why would I do this now in my old age? I went ahead and made the tea, went back to work and savored the ginger flavor.

As we grow in self-compassion, we watch what we apologize for and how often we do this. We maintain awareness of what draws forth anger and irritation toward ourselves. For example, some elders see their body as an enemy that fails them, instead of the awesome friend that it is. Our physical self has been good to us. For many years the complexity of cells, splendid organs such as kidneys, heart, and lungs have done their best, working as intended, keeping us alive and healthy. We can't prevent our physical self from wearing out any more than we can prevent an automobile driven for years with extensive miles to eventually sputter and cease working perfectly. As with a household appliance, our parts can be replaced only for so long until finally they become inoperable.

Our body has diligently worked for us and provided for our needs, but we hardly notice how good health has been maintained until certain segments begin to weaken and grow more unreliable. Now is the time to engage with our physical self by first thanking our body for the good it has done and continues to do for us. We gift our body with self-compassion when we tend to what our physical self requires for essential health: let a podiatrist cut our toenails; be sure to take our medications; do those exercises that medical professionals recommend; and, yes, eat healthily.

The same approach can be taken with our mind. Our brain has been remarkable in aiding our life, but this, too, gradually loses some of its previous effectiveness. Why would it be otherwise? Blaming ourselves for losing our balance, not remembering, or misplacing items only adds to a lack of a positive self-image, which then depletes more of our capacity to appreciate life. We are self-compassionate when we take part in activities that activate the brain and make an effort to keep learning and staying interested in topics that broaden our knowledge.

My hope for those of us who are older is that we will accept how aging pulls us out of our well-worn paths and slows us down. When we are self-compassionate, we patiently and kindly acknowledge this reality and refuse to blame ourselves for what is the natural process of all living beings who eventually move into the stage of old age.

# *Regret's Persistent Voice*

*You want to cry aloud for your*
*mistakes. But to tell the truth the world*
*doesn't need any more of that sound.*

~ Mary Oliver

The other night when I was having a conversation with friends, we spoke at a deeper level than about the weather or the latest sale items. We found ourselves marveling at how "life" led us to be the persons we are at our age. Before long, the word "regret" entered our exchange, as it tends to do when older people meander around in their personal stories. I've met very few who have not had at least one regret that won't leave them alone. More often, remorse about a number of things clings to memories of what has been—mistakes, unwise decisions, words expressed or unexpressed, relationships that could have been approached differently, life that might have been savored more.

Perhaps this surfacing of regrets results from visiting our memories more often in old age. The dross of our lived history is bound to gain our attention when we sort out the past to recall what we experienced and enjoyed. In one of his email messages, Ken (who is in his mid-nineties), confirmed this insistent pull that regrets have on us. Such angst travels beneath his words: “When we talked, you said you were writing a book about aging. One aspect you might consider is regrets. The longer I live, the more I feel sadness for some of the things I have done, as well as what I have failed to do.”

Ken’s message took me back to a day when I gave a presentation on grief. An older man stayed after the crowd went home to tell me what had happened to him the year before. With tears in his eyes, he described his wife’s journey with cancer and how he felt he had failed her. “She made it through the first two bouts with it, so when her third one came, I pushed her to live, constantly urging her to keep trying. She’d tell me she couldn’t do it anymore, but I didn’t listen to her.” He went on to explain his excruciating regret: “I was in denial that she was dying. Why didn’t I understand and accept that? Why didn’t I speak more gently to her? I wish I’d helped her more before she died.”

I felt this man’s cutting pain as he spoke, but I did not try to talk him out of it. Regret is not something one can take off like soiled clothes. These self-recriminations are like bedbugs, hard to get rid of. They bite into our mind and lead us away from an orientation toward peace. I assured him that I understood how heartache becomes intensified with remorse like his, that others have known something similar, that it is possible to move on from this misery, but that it takes time and self-forgiveness before being able to leave regrets behind.

When I hear elders talk about how they wish they had acted differently in their past, I’m especially sympathetic to that sorrow because of the nagging regrets that poked at me for a long time after my mother died. Even though we had a beautiful friendship, a wave of compunction swept me up and added to the grief. It took ten years before those remembrances no longer stabbed at my heart. I finally realized that if my failures had bothered my mother, she had long since forgiven me. It was myself that I had to forgive. This graced awareness led me to walk away from my regrets, although they still return occasionally to needle me. Each time they try to claim my peace, I deliberately shake them off. My mother died over twenty years ago and I am confident she would want me to focus on the love I have for her, which is much stronger than anything I failed to be or do.

Regret can involve more than feeling bad for our actions and negligence. It might include words and actions that brought harm to someone, not having developed certain talents that would have led to a more satisfying life for ourselves, or having missed opportunities to follow long-held dreams, such as risking adventures or traveling more.

Regrets in later years include decisions made to not accept a marriage proposal, while others who married may bemoan not choosing to bear children when they see the joy of their friends with grandchildren. Others regret having stayed for years at a job that yielded mostly misery. And then there are older people with poor health who keenly regret their years of smoking and excessive drinking.

Healing from our regrets includes encountering and giving them due attention. We begin by acknowledging what troubles us in this regard. What is the source of our concern? Was this deliberate on our part? We look closely to see if we actually failed or only assume we did because of unreasonable expectations of ourself or others. If we actually chose poorly or acted unfairly, we lament and grieve for what took place. And then we forgive ourselves.

There is a difference between regretting and lamenting. Lament expresses the pain and makes attempts to release it.

This crying out reaches toward healing the soreness and lessening its hold. Regret, on the other hand, nibbles away at the spirit, erases good memories, and refuses to stop jabbing us with disparagement and blame. Lament turns outward and liberates the pain; regret turns inward, clings to the pain, and refuses to be freed. As William Martin notes,

> . . . always wishing things
> had worked out differently
> withers our spirit
> and makes us older than we are.

Healing from regret includes being willing to welcome our less-than-perfect self back home into our heart, without excusing our mistakes but also not clinging to them. We may also have to forgive the person or the situation we were in at the time, to release our emotional response to what caused our failure to be who we wanted to be or do what we hoped to do. Clinging to regrets can suction out a lot of emotional energy. Why continue to give away this precious commodity? What good does it do to castigate ourselves for something we cannot undo? Why not direct our vitality to imbibing the joy of being alive and focus on the ways that we are loving, caring persons?

When regrets insist on chafing our spirit, we have the power to keep them from doing so. We can choose to stand up for the good person who lives inside us and move forward freed of those regrets. We can talk back to what eats away at our spirit. Freedom of mind and heart increases when we respond to our remorse with something like this: "That was then. This is now. I've learned. I am wiser. I'm leaving that part of my past behind."

# *The Healing Path*

*In our souls, as on the sea, storms subside gradually.*

~ Pierre Teilhard de Chardin

When elders enter the last decades, they do so with a certain amount of emotional and mental debris from the past blows of life, such as harsh work experiences, relationship skirmishes, old grudges, self-blame, or blaming God for tragedies that resulted in unresolved sorrow. Some may also be suffering from the devastation of shattering childhood ordeals. The wounded parts of ourselves do not mysteriously disappear when we are older. They may hide out better or underlie some other ache or pain that disturbs our physical self. We are never too old to require more healing from what holds our peace hostage.

When I read James Finley's tender and honest memoir of healing from childhood and young adult trauma, I noticed several foundational traits in *The Healing Path*. Finley tells us we do not always know our inner being is crying out for healing. If we do become aware of this, we aren't sure how to go about the mending. When we do finally find a way and a skilled counselor, it can take a long time to fully engage with what leads to inner peace.

Finley knows personally about healing from his own hidden wounds left unattended and the many years it took to heal from them. As a child, he was terrorized and traumatized by a drunken father, and then as a young adult he was sexually seduced and assaulted by a priest. It was years later when Finley was able to enter the healing path to personal freedom from that trauma. Only much later than that, now in his eighth decade, did he call forth the courage and vulnerability to reveal to his readers the painful process he deliberately chose in order to regain internal harmony.

A wound of any size left unattended influences the peace and freedom of old age. If we have grieving to do regarding hurts of the past, now is the time to address them directly. Just as our body indicates how to care for it—such as when to breathe, move, eat, and sleep—so, too, our spirit signals when it's time to acknowledge what ails and prevents us from being at home with ourselves. When hurtful memories keep barging into our thoughts, when we feel unsettled, or continually concerned about a past event, it may be that an unhealed wound is revealing itself and begging to be acknowledged and tended.

In Anne Rivers Siddons's novel, *Sweetwater Creek*, the wise housekeeper Cleta comforts twelve-year-old Emily after her frightening nightmare about being abandoned by her mother at the age of three years (which actually happened). Cleta tells Emily that it was more than a dream.

> "But we all knows down deep that it ain't nothin' but a big truth tryin' to catch up with you. You run, and it run harder. You turn and stare it down and it go slinkin' off like some ol' sissy. I seen it happen a lot of times."

As we grow old it's time to "stare down" what keeps us from peace. Face what still has its claws in us and unclench ourselves from it. Sometimes only when nearing the gate of death do people finally meet head-on what has been trying to catch up with them—such as no longer rejecting a beloved, forgiving an alienated son or daughter, reconciling with or leaving a harsh, rule-oriented church, or finally accepting the goodness resting at the core of one's being. Hopefully, we will not wait until that crucial last farewell before resolving what longs for resolution.

When deep-seated hurts surface, grief accompanies the awareness and the process of healing from them. No one wants to go through the messy emotional and mental disturbance of facing what caused us to hurt badly, but this precedes our healing. If we're willing to plow through the hardened crust of the past, a fresh landscape of equanimity can result. In *The Cure for Sorrow* Jan Richardson asks her readers to "remember that grieving is not an orderly process. Grief is the least linear thing I know. Hardly a tidy progression of stages, grief tends to be unruly." She then states a fact about grief that I believe to be especially relevant for older persons: "It [grief] spirals us back through layers of sorrow we thought we had dealt with." Those layers are what we uncover as we age. Each one we expose, explore, and deliberately choose to move beyond leads us farther along the path of peace.

Part of our healing process involves the wisdom and meaning we discover from having been wounded. For an older person, this is one of the benefits of looking back to mend what took place. With the distance between now and when we were hurt, our clarity grows in understanding how our woundedness led to spiritual growth, to becoming a better person. Perhaps this growth activated our compassion, or influenced our choice of a career in which others with a similar wounding could be assisted, or helped us become less judgmental and more understanding of others' behavior when they act out of their pain. Perhaps it was our wounding that convinced us of the power of leaning on a divine Presence that became our only consolation.

Something that has helped me to meet pieces of the unhealed past has been the assurance of my spirit's resilience. We all have more courage and strength within us than we realize. In *The Gold in Your Memories*, Macrina Wiederkehr attests to this gift in us:

> "Are you aware that there is a life in you that no one can destroy? Can you accept the truth that within you a thing of beauty is being kept safe for you? What is it that needs to be awakened or restored in you? . . . When you are able to make that journey through those undesired parts of your life, you will most likely discover that your inner strength has been leading you in ways you never dreamed."

Inner peace, increased empathy for the pain of others, plus a big step into freedom of mind and spirit make the journey into and out of our past wounds worth the effort. As poet Jennifer Jinks Hoffmann attests: "Allowing pain to run its course is holy work. . . . so when I stay with my suffering, when I keep praying to God from my broken heart, the Divine often feels closer to me."

May this be the reality for any and all of us when we choose to reach back and visit what pleads for healing.

# VI

# Gratitude

## "The Pulse of Positivity"

Sometimes you can almost touch it,
feel it absorbing your inmost being;
you sense the pulse of positivity
steadily thrumming in your old age.

You tumble and go crashing down
and someone comes to lift you up.
Loneliness haunts your empty heart
until grandchildren stop to visit.

Another ache in your arthritic joints
greets you when you slowly awaken,
but then you turn to see the sunrise
gloriously coloring the crimson sky.

You receive the dreaded message
of yet another loved one departing,

and a friend wraps her arms around you
offering consolation, promising presence.

The day stretches out long and slowly
but when eventide finally arrives
you trace the pattern of the past hours,
grateful for the good among not-so-good.

~ Joyce Rupp

# *Finding What Is Good*

*If you concentrate on finding whatever is good in every situation,*
*you will discover that your life will suddenly be filled with gratitude,*
*a feeling that nurtures the soul.*

~ Harold Kushner

Much has been written about the benefits of gratitude. While everyone profits from this essential approach to daily life, none more so than elders. Amid the aches and endless changes, we will find it valuable for our inner peace if we keep an eye on the positive.

In *Recipes for a Sacred Life,* Rivvy Neshama affirms the value of thankfulness: "Some people say that gratefulness is the key to a sacred life. Others say it is the key to happiness. There have even been studies that correlate gratitude with good health, less depression, and a good night's sleep." That's quite a promise, so why not be grateful? We can sit around and grouse about how miserable we feel, how many people we know who are ill or dying, and how wretched the world situation is, or we can perk up and look for what is good in what we have, and maybe even find something of value in what we perceive as the not-so-good.

Frank Cunningham comments, "Grateful people tolerate loss well by seeing the bad in the context of the larger good—the joy of life." This wise author of *Vesper Time* knows we can't "have it all." Oh, we might have it all for a brief while, but life is impermanent and things change, sometimes rapidly, because that is the nature of our existence. If having it all is our goal, we will often be discontent and disgruntled. It is to our benefit to be happy with what we have. We can still want our life to improve, but we try to be satisfied and accept what there is to be grateful for.

Being deliberate about looking for the good is essential if we are to discover reasons to give thanks. This is part of the wisdom of aging, knowing we will never have everything we want. Much that is worthwhile still belongs to us. If we just look—and sometimes we have to look quite intently—we will find the desirable nesting within the undesirable. When we review our personal history, we'll see that both the wanted and the unwanted traveled side by side with us most of the time. We rarely experienced all negative or all positive things. Usually daily life was a mix of both.

Macrina Wiederkehr was nearing eighty when she wrote in *Abide:*

> How often I moan and groan about something that has been taken away from me, failing to notice that I am utterly surrounded with gifts given. So often I do not see what is at my side, in my midst, in my heart! Sometimes it is a person that I fail to see. Sometimes it is the power of an experience that could be a healing force in my life if I would look at it with new eyes and allow it to be a moment of grace. There is much that I miss because I'm not

present with authenticity. My body is there but my mind is distracted. Thus I miss the time of grace.

We may be so absorbed in what we've left behind that we fail to appreciate what we've gained that can ease some of the liabilities of aging. Older persons in assisted living may not always have meals they enjoy, but they do not have to cook or clean up afterward. If no longer allowed to drive, they avoid the expense of caring for a car, along with concerns about traffic or possible accidents that could hurt themselves or others. Elders moving to a senior residence from a home they've lived in for years will not have to exert the effort in lawn care and other home upkeeping. Plus, they have new opportunities for an expanded social life.

The following lines from Naomi Shihab Nye's poem, "Half and Half" speak to how we can make the most of something worthwhile from the little we have:

> She is making a soup from what she had left
> in the bowl, the shriveled garlic and bent bean.
> She is leaving nothing out.

So, too, with us. For example, certain activities cost us in terms of our get-up-and-go when we agree to leave the comfort of our residence for any amount of extended time. If our energy feels more like a deflated balloon than a bouncy tennis ball after we've been on an outing, we consider what we gained at the cost of a bit of weariness—perhaps the joy of stimulating conversation with others, viewing something wondrous, or the pleasure of a delicious meal.

If we are to find what is good among the not-so-good, we will need to have patience with the time it takes to adjust to alterations in various aspects of our living. We look for sources of gratitude when the emptiness of what we no longer have assails us. Elders sometimes make the best of an uncomfortable situation by laughing at themselves. What is it about laughter that lightens the load weighing on our spirits?

Poet laureate Donald Hall did this when he received the coveted National Medal of Arts from President Obama. Hall reflected on his experience in *Essays After Eighty*:

> A military man took my arm to help me climb two stairs, as I had seen another do for Roy Acuff. I told the President how much I admired him. He hugged my shoulder and bent, speaking several sentences into my left ear, which is totally deaf. I heard nothing except my heart's pounding. After my friends watched on the Internet and saw the President address me, they asked what he had said. I told them that he said either "Your work is immeasurably great" or "All your stuff is disgusting crap," but I couldn't make out which.

We can grow in the habit of deliberately focusing on the positives rather than the negatives of old age. If we look only at what we do not want, the beauty, joy, and satisfaction will slip from our view. Finding the good in the not-so-good is something we can achieve as we continue to age. We keep practicing at it, choosing, as the ancient adage suggests, to *see the cup half full rather than half empty.* In doing so, we allow happiness and gratitude to claim a spacious area in our heart. We allow joy to be our companion on the journey of Elderhood.

# *Traces of the Past*

*They are campfires to return to over and over.*

~ Roger Housden

One summer evening I sat before a crackling campfire with several of my relatives. Easy conversation moved among us while darkness slowly descended and a full moon arrived with its bold rays of light. New and old stories filled us with laughter. A deep connection began to form among us, leaving me to marvel at the magic of a campfire to draw forth what rests in our memories. I felt like one of Steven Charleston's visitors, "Taking in his memories like food for the soul."

As I grow older, the advice in the Book of Deuteronomy becomes ever more important to me. "But take care and watch yourselves closely, so as neither to forget the things that your eyes have seen nor to let them slip from your mind all the days of your life; make them known to your children and your children's children" (Deuteronomy 4:8–9) We can't bring back our youth nor the wonderful parts of life that enriched us, but we can honor what they contributed. We gather what we enjoyed. We welcome the happenings that lifted our spirits. This assures us there is more glad than not glad in what we have known. Poetry editor Roger Housden suggests that we sit with a good poem the way one sits contemplatively before a campfire. I suggest we do the same with our engaging memories, allowing them to visit us with their warmth and consolation.

If we allow ourselves the time to reflect, the past will come to the surface with amazing swiftness. We need only ask ourselves a question such as "Who are the people who left me feeling enthused about life? What events sailed hope into my heart? What beautiful places that I've visited have captivated my wonder?" Usually one fruitful memory will generate another, our mind inevitably taking us along a river of gratitude.

These traces of the past include people, places, experiences, and events that left a beneficial imprint on our innermost self. Remembrance of them helps to balance the defeats and forfeitures that come naturally as aging progresses. Recollecting our bountiful memories not only elicits a sigh of satisfaction, it steers us away from falling into a mood of despondency. As Nancy Wood reminds us,

> Things that remember themselves give light
> to the uncertain paths we used to take,
> bringing beauty to the house
> of our ripening old age.

Cherished memories could leave us with a feeling of sadness, knowing we will be unable to repeat much of what brought us pleasure. We have a choice as to which way we turn our mind and heart when we opt to gather these remembrances. For instance, in my late seventies I wrote in my journal of how impossible it was to repeat the early morning mountain hikes I used to do:

> Nostalgia circles around inside, trying to woo my deeper self into longing for what cannot be. I forego that useless enticement and turn to collect some pleasing memories of lake and woods, stars still bright, those times when I stood in the pre-dawn with a silent, contemplative gaze, utterly amazed at what I beheld. Today in pre-dawn I recall how precious those times were. I sit with gratitude for my contented memories.

When we revisit prized people and situations within the context of our personal history, we find both inner strength and a clearer perception of how we currently know ourselves. Imagine an oak that has lived a long time. Think of its history. There's such grandeur in a tree's individual characteristics, the indications of how the oak became grounded and rooted in order to endure rough storms ripping through the branches. If the tree could speak of what brought joy, we would be hearing all kinds of mesmerizing stories—birds giving birth to their young, sunshine encouraging growth, leaves tickled by the wind and washed fresh by falling rains. We would also hear how the tree endured severe storms and dreadful lightning flashes.

So, too, with our lives woven with golden memories mixed in with the not-so-golden, at least, not golden in our perception. Yet, all these memories form "rings of growth," like those inside a tree. Imagine creating a concentric circle for each year of our lives. How many memories of how life shaped us would those lines contain?

I learned at an early age to value reflecting and reminiscing. The poet William Wordsworth was one of the first writers to awaken my heart to this. As a high school student I admired how he found depth-filled words to speak of the splendor and meaning in life. I noticed that it was Wordsworth's reflection on his experiences of the past that enabled him to find this splendor and meaning. He writes in "To the Daffodils" of seeing these beautiful flowers and then revisiting them in his memory:

> For oft, when on my couch I lie
> In vacant or in pensive mood,
> They flash upon that inward eye
> Which is the bliss of solitude

In other poems, Wordsworth's recollections make clear his belief that memory is

> a dwelling place
> For all sweet sounds and harmonies.

Memories continually arise from within us. In *Telling the Bees*, novelist Peggy Hesketh's character, Albert, sums up their presence this way: "I am an old man now, an old man whose memories pulse more strongly than the blood in my veins." So, too, with us. While we reminisce by the campfires of our inner self, the traces of the past that pulse in the veins of our aged life sustain us with their glad tidings.

# *Harvesting*

*Will we become sages,*
*harvesting the spiritual essence of our lives*
*and blessing all future generations?*
*Or will we just grow older,*
*withdrawing,*
*circling the wagons,*
*and waiting for the end?*

~ William Martin

My favorite season as a young person living on an Iowa farm was harvesting time. This was when the hard work of planting and cultivating the fields of corn, oats, and soybeans led to their final, matured stage. What joy of accomplishment to join in the gathering of ripened grains, to fill the wagons and bins with this abundance. Even now, if I happen to drive in a rural area when farmers are bringing in the harvest from their fields, my heart stirs in happy remembrance.

The concept of gratitude brings along with it the notion of harvesting—gathering what we have given ourselves to with dedication and determination—filling the bins of our heart with a plentitude of love in its varied facets, with the gratification of knowing that what we diligently tended with care and responsibility has yielded the worthy returns of matured perceptions and peacefulness.

Zalman Schachter-Shalomi describes his notion of harvesting as

> gathering in the fruits of a lifetime's experience and enjoying them in old age. . . . We consciously recognize and celebrate the contributions we have made in our career and family life. We also appreciate the friendships we have nurtured, the young people we have mentored, and our wider involvements on behalf of the community, the nation, and ultimately the Earth.

Perhaps another way to verbalize this would be to speak about "legacy"—the fruits of our lives that we hope to leave for the coming generations. What do we specifically include in that legacy? What might be helpful or supportive to those who live after us? Surely we would share the hard lessons we learned along the way when we went through rough stretches, aching for situations to end or turn in another direction. Our harvest also includes an integrity that has been yeasted with divine grace and enriched by our choices to be true to our authentic self. When they recognize how we have nurtured that integrity in ourselves, young people will be encouraged to trust in their own personal skills and spiritual growth.

Another feature of harvesting has to do with grandparenting. Connecting with grandchildren of any age is a way of expressing one's legacy, not just through spoken advice but also—and more importantly—through the way in which a grandparent believes in and accepts a grandchild by giving the generous gift of true attention and listening, being open to and accepting of the young person's character, enjoying shared outings—all these and other ways of creating "memory-making times" that can have an effect on a grandchild's future.

Harvesting cannot begin until we believe we have something to gather. This relies on the belief and conscious recognition that our lived experience contains worth, not just for self but for others. I fear that too many elders do not believe they have any significance. They do not trust they have anything that could make a difference, that would inspire others or be helpful for their future. Although these elders have tried to live their best, still the question *What have I done with my life that might influence others?* disheartens them. If these self-effacing elders do manage to find some meaningful aspects in their lives, they tend to ignore them by falling into the pit of a detrimental comparison with what others have accomplished. This leads to judging their contribution as pitifully small and unimportant.

I know this kind of response to harvesting happens. Thirty years ago I experienced life-altering counseling from a Jungian therapist. Rebecca led me through my midlife struggle and opened the door to a future expansion in personal transformation that I would never have achieved without her guidance. How saddened I was years later to receive a response to a letter I had written her when she was in her early eighties to thank her again for the incredible gift of her presence and skills in my younger years. In her return letter Rebecca told me of losses she had experienced a few years previously. This was followed by her shocking statement: "I sometimes wonder if I have ever done anything right." I wanted to cry out "Oh no!" to this woman who had helped me more than anyone else to take the risk in becoming who I am today. I've often wondered when it was that she stopped believing in her own gifts and legacy. I hope my letter to Rebecca made a difference and lifted her downcast spirit.

Doubting our ability to have made a difference could happen to any of us. It is a great comfort to have someone remind us of how positively we affected their life. Not long ago, a colleague of mine mentioned her friend who, she said, "has reached a point in his life in which he no longer can do what he used to love doing." She added, "It's a huge loss for him. One day he told me how people were thanking him for his influence and encouragement in their lives and I thought, *This is a time of harvest for him. The seeds of goodness he planted have grown and flourished. He's just now hearing about the bounty.*"

When we deliberately search for what has matured in us, and if we trust in its nature to positively affect others, we attest to our desire to leave something that will make a difference. As Nancy Wood wisely notes, "Change means growth. Growth is necessary for trees and other living things. Without growth, nothing would be harvested, except doubt."

We have grown and continue to grow. We gather not just from the past but from what is presently evolving in our lives. Here we continue to nurture our inherent goodness, rejoice in newly found relationships, maintain an openness to receive as well as to give, and sustain a daily effort to accept people whose beliefs and actions are different than ours.

Each of our lives contains something ripened and ready for harvesting. It is never too late to add to the bounty of this harvest.

# *Holding Out the Chalice*

*Each morning we must hold out*
*the chalice of our being*
*to receive, to carry, and to give back.*

~ Dag Hammarskjold

Gratitude gently moves us toward being generative. The more we acknowledge how much has been bestowed to us, the better motivated we are to share from the chalice of our fullness. Each morning I close my meditation time with a prayer of the Indian philosopher Shantideva that expresses a desire to lessen the suffering of those in the wider world. One line of the prayer calls me to be generous with what I have been given. The words are few, the intention enormous: *May I be a vase of plenty.* This brief statement reminds me that the plenitude I've received is not for my sake only. Much has been poured into the chalice of my being and much is to be emptied from it to benefit humankind.

Lewis Richmond detected this natural inclination to pour from the chalice of our abundance when he wrote,

> To help others when they are in need is so natural that we rarely stop to think about the full scope of

> its benefits. Helping others brings out the best in us at any age, but as we grow older, helping takes on an additional coloration and value. We begin to experience it more not just as helping, but as *giving back*. As life progresses into middle and old age, we come to feel that this life is a gift that we yearn to repay.

In Elderhood, we make a special effort to "pay it forward," sharing what we have received. When society looks upon older people as having nothing further to give, seeing them capable of only receiving, then everyone misses the gifts of gratitude. Even if a person is confined or physically infirm, the chalice of the heart always has something to be poured out, something worthwhile to contribute. The vessel of old age most certainly contains much appreciation for personal care, spilling over with smiling eyes for each visitor and helpful attendant. Always the chalice can hold out the support of prayerful abiding.

Other chalices of older people overflow with specific talents they are still able to share. Those adept at using computers and electronic devices come to the assistance of persons having difficulty using them. Elders who continue to drive make it a habit to bring along a non-driver to the supermarket. It matters little what kind of abundance fills the chalice of our hearts. We need only have the intent, desire, and willingness to do as Nicki Verploegen suggests in *Give Us This Day*: "*Spend your heart*. That's what I heard when waffling over how much of myself to give to some difficult projects."

Pouring from the chalice of our abundance is somewhat like presenting the beneficial parts of who we are—

the blessings, good fortune, and enrichments we choose to share in our elder years in hope of positively touching the life of another. Our filled chalices are probably not earth-shattering, but we have things we trust can live on as an encouragement for someone in need of what we are offering. I found this inconspicuous generativity one summer in an aunt and uncle who had arrived in the city for a gathering of their extended family of children, their spouses, and grandchildren. They were in their mid-nineties, and the trip had involved strenuous effort on their part. Travel meant leaving their home in the northwest U.S. before dawn to catch a flight that was considerably delayed before departing for the Midwest. There was also a stopover in another busy airport. My uncle's legs had weakened a lot, causing every step to be cautious and painful. My aunt's recent back surgery left her relying on a walker. This journey was not meant for the faint-of-heart. They poured their precious energy and love from their aged chalices. This is what I envision the generativity of Elderhood to be. This aged couple wanted to be with their family. They had made the difficult journey knowing that it would be their farewell to a beloved son-in-law about to enter hospice. I thought of the magnificence of giving themselves so fully, how the kindness and generous love in their beings flowed out into those who had gathered, to be lived on in that generation long after these grandparents were deceased.

If we doubt we have anything of value in our chalice to give, we need only to read what Steven Charleston points out in *Ladder to the Light*:

> Look at all the good you have done, little by little, person by person, over all these years, with every

> helping act you performed, with every kind word you spoke. The Spirit says, "I know you want to offer a disclaimer, but your mistakes do not erase the good. Over all these years, you have been a channel of grace, a source of healing, a friend in need. You have acted from a deep sense of compassion. You have sacrificed for the sake of others, I do not remind you of this out of some sense of false flattery, but only to acknowledge a simple truth: if every bit of good you have done were a grain of sand, you would be standing on a beach."

Think of the joy and gratification you feel when you have gone beyond self, when you have chosen to be of service in some way, sharing from what you received in the past. As Steven Charleston suggests, even self-giving the size of a grain of sand has an effect—like choosing to greet a stranger with a cheery "good morning" when you feel out of sorts and then receiving an even bigger joyful greeting back, one that sends your spirit humming for the rest of the day. This circle of generativity is reflected in a segment of the familiar prayer attributed to St. Francis of Assisi: "*It is in giving that we receive.*"

How marvelous it would be if we poured from our interior chalice with the enthusiasm of lily pods whose sturdy black seeds pop open and spring forth with a jack-in-the-box quickness. Just one touch of a finger, the brief landing of a bird, a strong wind, or the bumping of a neighborly plant sends the generative seeds flying forth when they are mature.

Like lily pods giving away the potential for new flowers to grow, we elders allow our ripened goodness and giftedness to pour forth from us.

VII

# Physical Decline

## "Bent-over Elders"

Walking up the hill I passed an old oak
bending gracefully over the sidewalk,
strong winds or some genetic mishap
curving her tall trunk further every year
until she now lends shelter and shade
to all who make their way upon the path.

Older persons whose bending bodies
press their faces downward, shoulders
rounded, pulled toward the ground—
I've not, until now, noticed the silent grace
in the strong leaning of these bent bodies,
only felt what must be the inflexible effort
to look upward at another in conversation,
to walk forward, unseeing, and unaware
of what obstacle might become a barrier.

Not until now have I appreciated the sight,
how an aging, bent-over elder portrays
an unspoken metaphor of inner strength.
Like an old oak giving shade to passersby,
so the elder with bowed head of acceptance,
still singing glad songs of wit and wisdom,
still rejoicing spirits with gracious presence,
still giving of one's self to generating love.

~ Joyce Rupp

# *Physical Ailments*

*Cruel night sneaks in, breaks*
*the locks of my weakened body,*
*penetrates, and takes my pride.*

~ Rabindranath Tagore

While I'm sitting in the booth for lunch with friends my age, I feel this throbbing in my upper thigh and think, "Now what is *that*? What is running awry there? Could a blood vessel be breaking?" I unobtrusively put my hand on my thigh, thinking, "I'd better pay attention to this." As my hand touches my thigh, it dawns on me that I have my mobile phone on vibrate in my pants' pocket and a call is coming in. Hilarious, eh? A reminder that underneath the surface of the calm acceptance I usually have regarding my health, this voice lurks: Be aware. *Anything* can happen *at any time* to *any part* of your body or mind.

I used to wonder why older people constantly talked about hips and heart, bladder and bunions, eyes and ears, what meds they took for this and that, and how much of each. But when you have constant pain, loss of major areas of independence, or a sizeable portion of the morning consumed in convincing your joints and hands to move, at least enough to get dressed, why wouldn't the focus be on what ails, hurts, and holds no promise of ending? Now I understand why, with less to occupy one's mind and no distraction of constant work, emerging physical ailments tend to take over for some elders. Yet, I've also known older folks with a lot of health concerns who choose to rarely bring these into their chats, remaining cheerfully connected to what's happening beyond themselves.

In her mid-eighties, anthropologist and primatologist Jane Goodall spoke to Douglas Abrams about a serious fall she'd taken. She dismissed the problems associated with it: "So many older people I knew spent a great deal of time focused on their aches and pains, but those who seemed healthiest and happy were those who focused on something beyond their own troubles." Goodall didn't deny the misfortune of the accident, but her chosen attitude enabled her to cheerfully continue her compassionate work.

One characteristic clearly defining men and women in the last decades involves how quickly physical health can take a turn. On certain days arthritic aches intensify or sciatica strikes with a vengeance. Lower back spasms suddenly reoccur. Or with a few bites of the wrong food an old ulcer flares up, or a tooth breaks off. Such things are to be expected as the body and mind age, but our human psyche tends to assume we will be the exception.

The year of my eightieth birthday when I went for my annual physical check-up, Dr. Eric Holm entered the room holding up my medical chart and greeted me with "Hello Miss Healthy." I told him I could describe various brief encounters with bodily twinges but there was no need to worry because I felt in good shape. Alas, a few weeks after that visit, dreaded Covid caught up with me. A week in bed and more than two months of feeling energyless, I questioned whether I would ever regain strength. Fortunately, I bounced back. But I learned how abruptly one's good health can hit a scary pothole on the road.

While not denying the problems our good health may have, more persons in their eighties and nineties are thriving because they've kept their minds and hearts open, properly attended to their bodies, and maintained an interest in the global community. But just because I've taken good care of my health doesn't guarantee I'll avoid the body's decline. Some few older people *do* get to be frisky and unclaimed by illness until their final days, but most of us will slowly weaken and eventually leave the tree of life in the manner of autumn leaves. We would be wise to care well for our body and mind. There are elders who tune out doctors' instructions for daily exercise, will not eliminate certain foods in their diet, or will not take prescribed medications. Failing to follow through with such recommendations destroys physical health much sooner and works against being a person of good cheer.

When physical changes happen, we might consider our body as betraying us, but our body is simply following the process of a living organism—what all of creation experiences—vibrant health, then gradual deterioration that leads to subsequent physical mortality.

I like Susan Moon's attitude:

> My knees talk to me, and I have to respond. The old bones provide a kind of companionship. It's not really me who needs things like handrails and hiking poles, it's my knees. I make the arrangement for them, because we're family.

Along with caring for our health, we have to be our own advocate. We stand up for ourselves and do not allow medical personnel or systems to dismiss us and our health issues as non-essential by continuing to prescribe more and more pills, rather than being genuinely interested in searching for underlying causes and effective treatments.

I hope to maintain the attitude toward my physical decline that nature writer and environmentalist Barry Lopez describes in his book *Embrace Fearlessly the Burning World*:

> Most days I walk down to the river to say my prayers, but stiffened joints no longer allow me to walk the woods every day, and so I miss a lot. But I am comfortable here, even as the particularity of my knowledge of this landscape shrinks. If I hear the crack of a limb breaking, and the limb crashing through the canopy, the whump as it hits the forest floor, I think: Me, too. If I see a fledgling osprey drop a writhing fish it has caught because it's too heavy and then try to regain its place in the air, I think: I've done that. . . . For now, I sit outside in the evening and in the middle of the day and am not afraid of the unknown.

Health in old age is like being on a hike in the mountains where we meet obstacles such as flooded creeks, steep climbs, and the possibility of dangerous snakes, bears, and cougars. But this does not dim the views of awesome beauty along the way when we pause to notice them, nor does it lessen the wonder of breathing and being alive.

# *Hands Tell the Tale*

*those hard old hands that lay curled and still*
*near the soft gray felt hat on the table.*

~ Ted Kooser

One morning I met a friend for coffee. As we chatted about "aging" and how we were currently adjusting to the changes, he held out his long-fingered, knobby-arthritic hands. "Look at these. They don't lie," he announced while he spread his fingers as wide as they would go. I then placed my smaller, brown-splotched hands on the table opposite his. The veins on all four of our hands were not only visible, they looked like thick purple rivers inside papery skin. If we ever doubted we had joined the league of old folks, those hands convinced us of our membership.

Every once in a while I notice someone my age whose hands are free from blotches and blemishes and I wonder how that person can be so lucky to have clear skin. But then I catch my self-deprecating judgment and return to appreciating my hands for what they can still do. I remind myself that my hands have no need to look like someone else's. They are *my* hands. What a gift they've been, and are, for meeting my daily needs.

We can be quickly reminded we are old. We wake up one morning, go into the bathroom, look in the mirror as we're brushing our teeth. All of a sudden we see a new wrinkle and wonder, "When did *that* happen? It wasn't there yesterday." Then we notice a dangling hair growing underneath our chin or a long one sticking out of our ear. These unwanted visitors jolt us with their bold arrival in our younger years, but in later life we no longer consider their appearance on our body to be abnormal.

When we look at our reflection, we see an old face looking back at us. How do we accept that? How to be at home with facial features continually changing, perhaps looking a bit different every week, maybe oftener. Can we smile at the person who's shining through that wrinkled skin or do we turn aside with a grunt of aversion?

If we are feeling uneasy or disgusted about our bodily flaws and limitations owing to age, we may find ourselves easily making comparisons. And what is the value of that? Not much. Only that we probably think less of our own physical being, or bask in the ego's sunshine if we're "looking young."

Our bodies cannot stay as they were in our youth. Not even if we are a famous television personality at age eighty-one posing prettily for a national magazine. I looked at her photo on my newsfeed and thought, "How much Botox and plastic surgery, how many expensive creams did it require for her to look like that? It must have taken her make-up artist and hair dresser quite a bit of time to prep her for the photo, which is undoubtedly photoshopped." Then I caught my negative thinking. Not only was I making comparisons but I was also spitting out some "body-envy," wanting to make myself feel less unattractive by putting down someone who chose to make every effort into looking "young and beautiful."

At a meeting I attended, a sixty-five-year-old joked about older people who are "dripping, drooping, and dropping." Everyone laughed, including me, but on the way home I felt sad at that despicable description. The disparaging comment added to the negativity associated with the bodily alterations of elders. No wonder we look in the mirror and gasp in dismay at the image we see, instead of smiling at the loving person within that body.

I've long admired Albert Schweitzer, a compassionate humanitarian, wise philosopher, and dedicated physician. How surprised I was to read in *The Zen of Seeing* that artist Frederick Franck created a portrait of the eighty-six-year-old. Franck mentions that "Schweitzer became indignant when he noticed I was drawing him with his glasses on." Schweitzer protested, "*Don't, please, they make me look so old!*" You're probably smiling at this humanitarian's surprising vanity, but I am quite certain that most of us have a concern about "how old" we look when we arrive at our winter season.

If only we could accept the maxim that "No one sews a piece of unshrunken cloth on an old cloak; otherwise, the patch pulls away from it, the new from the old, and a worse tear is made" (Mark 2:21).Why do I think certain things shouldn't wear out if I take good care of them? Favorite clothes, the leather cover on my iPad—eventually they show how much they've been used—a frayed sleeve, small cracks on the cover—why not expect the same will happen with my body no matter the amount of healthful attention I provide? If only we could encourage one another to be content with the old cloak, to wear it proudly, graciously, without apology or disdain. If only we would refuse the culture's insistence on canonizing youthfulness and scorning the look of old age.

Eknath Easwaran offers encouraging words in *The End of Sorrow* about the effect of accepting our physical appearance:

> Such is the paradox of life: when we cling to the body, it loses its beauty, but when we do not cling to it, and use the body as an instrument given to us to serve others, even on the physical level it glows with health and beauty, as we can see from the lives of many mystics.

The *health and beauty* Easwaran refers to is not that which our Western culture adores. It is the beauty within, a radiance emitting a quiet glow in an elder.

I do not consider myself a mystic, but I do think positively about these purple-veined and blotchy hands of mine—how they continue to assist me in driving to visit homebound friends, writing a note for a celebration or sending a sympathy card, making soup for the ill, and carrying out other acts of service and kind-heartedness. How grateful I am for my hands that tell the tale of how old I am.

# *Climbing the Ladder*

> *Haywood and I are old enough now that we should really think twice before climbing the ladder into that attic.*
>
> ~ Margaret Renkl

At age seventy-eight, when renowned Florida photographer Clyde Butcher was featured in the AARP magazine, he reflected on his physical decline:

> Mentally I don't feel old, but physically it is a different story. After my stroke, I couldn't even get into a wheelchair at first. After six months, I was on a walker. I've taken that walker over rocks and logs, into the ocean and the swamp. It is thrilling. Nature fills you with vitality.

Butcher's approach to "carrying on" in spite of disability is amazing, but not every elder's physical change results in such a recovery or capability.

"Getting old" insists on our slowing down, doing less with greater effort, choosing more carefully how we siphon our energy. I noticed this a few years ago when I walked behind a gray-haired woman at the supermarket. As she carried her groceries out, she plodded at an excruciatingly slow pace. I pulled myself back like a rider yanking on the reins of a spirited horse. I was in a hurry, but I deliberately stayed back to show respect and not rush her. As she neared her car, the older woman turned around and said, "Thank you." I was moved by how humbly she acknowledged her slow-moving gait.

Poet Jennifer (Jinks) Hoffman admits, "In these later years of our lives, Alan and I speak frequently of our less-than-agile navigation of life, our physical pain, the diminishments that accrue with aging." She then adds a bit of humor: "These losses are the subject of many conversations we have with each other and our friends. *Organ recitals*, we sometimes joke. Our children witness us a little reduced and don't much like it, just as we felt when our parents aged and then died."

Let's be honest. No matter how much positivity we have, we're still going to lose some of our stamina. While this does not mean we have to meet this fate with a loss of hope or a disconnect with life, it does suggest the need for an acceptance of our waning energy. Not only do our bodies shrink in size, so does inner dynamism. We weary and wear out faster as the years sprint by. Given the unwanted changes with time hurrying us along, and our bodies balking at that hurrying, I understand the quip Gregory Boyle includes in *The Whole Language*:

> A Jesuit friend of mine went to a huge party for his grandfather who . . . turned one hundred. . . . The old man himself got up to speak at the end of a very long evening. He made his way slowly to the mi-

crophone and surveyed the room. This was all he had to say: *If you're given the chance to die in your seventies, take it. Thank you very much.*

I do not know if this man was making light of his increasing frailty or if he meant he'd rather have been dead thirty years earlier. He most surely referenced the inherent impoverishment that comes with the last decades. A few folks like Moses apparently never wearied. He's described as living to be "one hundred twenty years old when he died; his sight was unimpaired and his vigor had not abated" (Deuteronomy 34:7). Who of us in our late decades would not want that kind of potency? A few folks do remain extremely active well into their nineties, but the majority of us will feel the gradual degeneration of inner and outer strength in a body no longer complying with our demands and desires. It's useless to compare whether the weakening of my aging body is happening faster or slower than that of others. Weaken, it will.

While our bodies gradually fade, this depletion allows us an opportunity to develop a life vastly enriched and more meaningful than when life consisted of constant speed. We can find comfort in knowing that a lessening of strength and increasing frailty come naturally with the final years.

Like an old motor whose gears have grown sluggish, rusty, and worn thin from years of use, our body has come to the place where slowing down is not an option but a necessity.

Who of us has not known in ourself or in others something akin to what novelist William Kent Krueger describes through his central character, Frank, in *Ordinary Grace*:

> This year my father is waiting for me in the shade, sitting patiently on the porch of his condominium in Saint Paul, staring at the world from under the brim of a clean white ball cap. A tall man, slender all his life, he's grown thin and fragile over the last few years, with a heart that worries us both. I pull into the drive. He rises from the bench and hobbles to my car. He walks like a man built of toothpicks, afraid that the connection will not hold. He opens the door and eases this body, this awkward construction of brittle bone and loose flesh, into the passenger side. . . . "Good afternoon, sir," he says with chipper energy, and he gives me a smile, telling me with that flash of stained enamel that he's happy to see both me and another day.

And that is it—to be happy for another day of life. Whether we feel weak or strong as we move through the day, we can value our eldering self, much like Gunilla Norris summarizes the final years: "Even when we are old and can only smile and breathe, our worth extends into hidden places beyond our knowing. Our worth is not ours. It belongs to Life. We are its treasures."

# *When Things Fall Apart*

*Everyone is afraid of vulnerability, of falling.*
*Losing one's dignity is only the half of it.*
*No one wants to lose control.*

~ Emilie Griffin

A newborn is completely at the mercy of those who provide for the infant's basic needs. In old age, this kind of utter dependency can also occur before succumbing to death. For those who manage to escape a lengthy, vulnerable situation, they will still encounter reliance on others in the dying process unless a heart attack, accident, or other event causes instant death. Few elders escape some portion of old age's vulnerability.

If we have a medical procedure such as a colonoscopy or eye cataract surgery, the medical system will insist we have a driver to take us to and from the appointment. This is not a difficult requirement, but asking someone to be the required driver hints at a future when we will no longer have the ability to drive a car, ride a bicycle, or even walk.

No matter how much we try to hold everything together, in Elderhood things can quickly fall apart. One day my older sister had excellent health. The next day my brother-in-law was rushing her to the ER with concern for a possible heart attack. Our physical health supplies plenty of opportunities for this quick change in bodily functioning. Whether it is a debilitating stroke, loss of hearing or eyesight, increasing incontinence, a broken hip, cancer, or an incurable disease, some sort of challenge eventually reaches most everyone. If you've ever tripped on a curb, resulting in broken glasses, a smashed nose, and eyes ringed black as a raccoon's, you know about things rapidly falling apart.

Not only our bodies but our egos suffer from the surprise of physical mishaps that test our durability and undermine our self-confidence. Sooner or later we will meet that unsought moment when our tight hold on independence requires letting it slip into depending on someone or something else. This might be a caregiver, a physical prop such as a cane, walker, or wheelchair, or taking medications to regulate blood pressure or diabetes.

Depending on our personality, these developments expose a little or a lot of our personal defenselessness. Being the ultra-independent person I am, all kinds of feeling-words arise when I consider what this might mean for myself: *scary, risky, open to hurt, dependent, allowing another to take charge, losing control, giving in, feeling like a child, unable to be my own advocate, succumbing to another's way of doing things, dread, helplessness.* But then I remember compassion for self and kinship with others and am assured that I am not alone if I feel this way. Others have faced situations of greater magnitude that led to feeling inept, but they eventually recouped inner strength. I've observed resilient elders move beyond a struggle to accept what they can no longer do by themselves and proceed to make friends with their inabilities. Their experience tells me that I will be able to respond in a way that lessens the intensity of powerlessness when my time comes.

We must prepare ourselves for when we become increasingly dependent for our physical care. We do so now by being gracious and accepting of assistance when it is offered. At the same time, we do as much as we can for ourselves so as not to rely on others before this help is essential. I recall my mother telling me, "Don't do everything for me. I feel good when I can do something for myself." How right she was about having a balance between consenting to assistance and making an effort to manage on our own.

*When Things Fall Apart* is a book I often return to. My courage revives due to Pema Chodron's honesty about her exposure to being vulnerable, especially when she says, "All the ways I shield myself, all the ways I delude myself, all the ways I maintain my well-polished self-image—all of it fell apart. No matter how hard I tried, I couldn't manipulate the situation."

In writing about a difficult life-transition, Chodron admits how much it hurts "when the bottom falls out and we can't find anything to grasp." Fortunately, this Buddhist nun could see beneath what she experienced and she moved toward something that allowed her self-confidence to prevail:

> When things are shaky and nothing is working, we might realize that we are on the verge of something. We might realize that this is a very vulnerable and tender place, and that tenderness can go either way. We can shut down and feel resentful or we can touch in on that throbbing quality.

This "throbbing quality" refers to personal growth, an advancement in quieting the ego's insistence that we retain our independence, regardless of the cost to self or others.

Old age humbles us. After Missy Buchanan's health reached the stage of using a walker, she commented in one of her prayers for older adults, "I thought I was too old to learn anything new. I was wrong. I had to practice turning and parking again and again." Adding a bit of humor with that metaphor takes the edge off of accepting the humble use of a walker, but it does not remove the sense of limitations that comes with each step taken.

We ought not to conclude that being humbled has to knock us down and keep us there. As we proceed further into Elderhood, the alterations and significant adjustments we are forced to make contain the potential for our becoming more loving human beings. When renowned psychologist Robert Wicks writes about aging, he terms it "the wisdom years . . . that period of time when we take knowledge and add humility to sense life in a qualitatively different way." Wicks explains further, "When you take knowledge and you add humility, you get wisdom. And when that wisdom is added to compassion, you get love and such love is at the heart of a rewarding life."

Sometimes we simply have to take a deep breath, swallow hard, and talk to the part of our self that wants to believe we can do anything if we just exert enough effort. Depending on how self-willed and in control we have been earlier in life, it may be that only daily practice at being humble and a hefty amount of prayer will move us to accept the inevitable position of not being able to manage everything on our own.

Being humbled by Elderhood's requirements does not have to decimate our inherent joy or extinguish our love. Not if we understand what is truly of value.

# VIII

# DEATH

## "Prepared for Departure"

Here in the armchair of my final years,
I'm ready, waiting for the final call
to take off into Mystery.
A one-way ticket with my name
in permanent ink
is available at the imminent sign of departure.
The passport has been renewed and revised,
a mirror, not a photo, reveals my inmost self.
The suitcase of life sits emptied of
material values yet it barely closes,
filled to overflowing with integrity,
acceptance, and layers of kindness.

While I await the inevitable signal
to be on the way,

I finger the jeweled beads
of my lengthy history,
each one holds a memory, a gratitude, a prayer.
I breathe in the welcoming presence
of Forever-Love,
the tender, eternal companion
of my windowed soul.

With preparations assuring my readiness
near completion,
I ease into calm anticipation
of the future expedition.

~ Joyce Rupp

# *Dreaded Enemy or Liberating Guide*

> *We frequently talk of death,*
> *for we are very alert to the experience*
> *of the unknown that may be so near*
> *and it is only to those of one's own age*
> *that one can speak frankly.*
>
> ~ Florida Scott-Maxwell

A year before I entered into my eighth decade, I wrote in my journal:

> I want to come to terms with Death. People whose life I value keep dying. Eventually I'll have my own leave-taking. Perhaps Death does not snatch, cheat, or carry us away as often described. Maybe when that final breath nears, Death comes as a liberating guardian with gentle wings, a soft voice, a sweet word of welcome. I want to see Death, not as my enemy, but as a calm carrier through the shadowy passageway into future splendor.

For several years now I have repeated this affirmation: *I accept what my aging implies—farewells, endings, and eventually my own death.* I have come to terms with my departure, although I still hope it arrives years from now. Being with a number of dying people led me to acknowledge my resistance and stiff limitations of dread regarding mortality. I've concluded that if I detach from my old views, I'll have the courage required when it's my time to be unchained from what have been the taut bindings of my earthly security. Although I occasionally have times of hesitation, I do believe death can release me into the vast heart of Endless Love, guiding my freed spirit into a welcoming embrace.

The death of people who've found a home in my heart still challenges my acceptance of our earthly impermanence. Western society's negative view regarding mortality occasionally impinges upon my peacefulness. Will this visitor portrayed with skeleton and sickle ever be viewed as a guide leading through a gate of freedom, releasing what has, until now, been an impassable confinement of the soul?

Younger people understandably view death as a dreaded enemy that defeats life. Even for someone approaching eighty years or later, there's still a strong desire for life to go on and on. Anyone who's in reasonably good health won't be cozying up to death. But when diminishments raid the body and mind of their proficiencies, the reality of dying can no longer be viewed from afar.

"Death is the elephant in the room," writes Frank Ostaseski. "A truth we all know but agree not to talk about. We try to keep it at arm's length. We project our worst fears onto it, joke about it, attempt to manage it with euphemisms, side-step it when possible, or avoid the conversation altogether." The thought of their own death frightens some elders. My colleague Roseann discovered this in trying to organize a program for older men and women in religious communities, hoping for them to be "compassionate companions" for patients dying without family or friends. To Roseann's astonishment, most refused her invitation because of their discomfort at being around someone else's death, a reminder of their own.

No one knows definitely what might exist in "the hereafter," but what if society could view our physical ending as one that carries us into a fuller way of life. Hospice director Joyce Hutchison encouraged me to not fear death, to approach it positively as "another birthing." She suggested that when we were in our mother's womb we had no idea of what life would be like outside that nurturing, safe space. We may well have been terrified when bursting forth from that dark enclosure. Similar to human birthing, death's contractions will thrust us into another form of equally amazing life.

Like Joyce Hutchison, others have attempted to positively visualize "the beyond"—such as by visualizing it as going through pearly gates to meet their Maker, an unending banquet feast, golfing with buddies, being welcomed by a crowd of loved ones, dissolved into radiant Light, embraced by an unconditional Love, or simply being happy wherever "there" might be. Eknath Easwaran attests to this hope when he reminds his readers in *The End of Sorrow* that "even though we cannot but grieve when our dear ones pass away, the mystics tell us that underneath this grief we should always remember that death is only a change of rooms."

One morning when our women's group met, I invited us to reflect on this question: *What one sentence would you like to hear coming to you from the universe?* What I heard within myself was: *There's much more beyond your current life than you could ever dream possible.* What comfort and reassurance rested in that message. My hope stays strong in a future, positive sphere of existence. I believe this because of past experiences with dying persons.

Some of these experiences came during my years of volunteering with hospice. Quite a few dying patients saw "an angel" in the corner of a particular room. A few hours before my unconscious brother-in-law died, he opened his eyes wide and focused intently on something or someone none of us around his bed could see. A publisher's dying son described seeing vivid colors and hearing exquisite music before his death. A Catholic deacon, unable to speak, awakened briefly and marveled aloud, "It's so beautiful." He died the next day. Then there's the terminally ill nun in a coma who lifted her head up from the pillow, sat up, stretched her arms wide, and exclaimed, "Here I am. Take me! Take me!" She fell back, exhaled one last breath, and was gone.

I've learned that death is to be respected. It has its own timetable, its own rhythm, its own heartbeat. Those whom I've accompanied as death neared often ask, "How will I know?" I assure them, "I don't know, but what I do know is that *you* will recognize death's call. I've observed this time and again. Something within taps the soul and beckons, and you'll realize it is time to depart. Give yourself into the mystery of what awaits beyond this earthly sojourn. Trust that you'll know and have the courage to do what is needed."

We have a choice to see death as a frightening enemy or as a friendly visitor arriving to calmly bear us into another sphere of existence. There is no need to fear death. Neither is there a need to hurry its arrival nor to fight it off. Death will come when it is our turn to depart. Whether this comes swiftly and unforeseen, or in an agonizingly slow period of waiting, we give ourselves to embracing what is beautiful, good, and true beyond the life we cherished.

# *Like a Shooting Star*

*I'm not going to die, honey.*
*I'm going home like a shooting star.*

~ Sojourner Truth

How many of us when we speak about death—our own or someone else's—would consider death to be the shooting star that Sojourner Truth envisioned? She had an extremely tough life during which she was bought and sold as a slave numerous times. Eventually freed, she became a preacher against slavery and later spoke out for women's rights. At age eighty-six, shortly before she died, Sojourner still carried a bold hope in her faith-filled heart when she made that statement about her death. I've never envisioned my death to be like Sojourner's, but I *have* arrived at a hopeful and satisfying view of it. This came about, as difficult truths often do, only after a surprising and disturbing incident.

When I reached my early sixties, I thought I was at peace with my eventual death, accepting what the author of the Book of Sirach writes, "All living beings become old like a garment, for the decree from of old is, 'you must die'" (14:17–19). I'd witnessed some truly touching deathbed scenes of patients and loved ones. So it came as a bit of a shock to grasp the fact that there was another part to my death I had not accepted. I still had to learn how to be at home with what might happen *after* my death.

This awareness came while I was making a private, week-long retreat at a wonderful place of breathtaking beauty and solitude. My cabin rested within a grove of birch trees beside a crystal-clear lake that easily allowed for a spirit of peacefulness. One evening I went outside with the intention of enjoying a sky crowded with starry constellations. At first when I rested on my back on the dock, I felt intense awe at the light-filled glory. But then a menacing-looking, murky cloud floated overhead. As the cloud passed over me, a fear-filled dread took over. I was completely undone by the reality of my apparent nothingness.

I lay there consumed with the thought that I was only an infinitesimal speck in an expanding and immeasurable universe. The same words kept repeating in my mind: *Nothing. I will consist of nothing after I die.* I could not bear the thought so I leapt up and raced back inside the cabin, shaken to my core. When I returned home, I buried the experience inside myself, choosing to mentally and emotionally disassociate with what had taken place. And I stopped deliberately gazing at the stars, even though I'd always felt drawn to them.

Seventeen years later, while attending a conference honoring cultural historian Thomas Berry on his tenth anniversary of death, this terror finally dissolved. During one of the presentations, a speaker mentioned having asked Thomas Berry where he thought he might be after he died. To my graced amazement, here is what ninety-three-year old Berry replied: "*I'll be where I've always been—in the universe.*" Such a simple and apt response, one that finally ended my fear. Everything I'd struggled with about my becoming nothing became almost instantly clear. Because of research and studies, I knew my body was made of stardust, but I never made the connection of those elements in myself always remaining someplace in the universe after I died. I found peace from Berry's response, knowing that whatever form "I" will have, I'll always be within the magnificent vastness that I gazed on while lying on the dock that disturbing night. My physical self, in whatever form it evolves into—soil, air, vegetation—will be a part of planet Earth circling in the sun in our Milky Way Galaxy. My spirit, my essence, will be free to float among the starlit cosmos.

I continue to find consolation and assurance about the afterlife in comments by wise persons like the Dalai Lama. When the Dalai Lama was asked what he thought would happen to him after death, he shrugged and, with his usual contagious laughter, offered three words: "Change of clothing." A Hindu philosophy approaches aging and death as that of a jacket wearing out, with it eventually needing to be thrown away. When we reach Elderhood with its increasing physical degeneration, it's not surprising that we might wish to be freed of the physical self. Who wouldn't want a sending off to be like the dazzling light of a comet, or maybe the freedom suggested in *The Seventh Book of Wonders* where Julianna Baggott tells her readers, "I feel death inside of me now. It's not far off. But sometimes death feels like the wings of a goose—sturdy, broad, a sloping lawn before me, the possibility of flight."

Comments like these strengthen my belief that I do not have to wait until "eternity" for a profound unity with the

Great Mystery, nor do I need to fear what happens when I die. Even now, in my earthly, solid robe, my "I" intertwines with the grand universe. When I leave this physical clothing of self behind, my spirit will be free to sail within the universe, in union with the Maker of Stars from whom my dusty self came into being.

I may not feel like Sojourner Truth's shooting star when I'm dying. I might feel more like the last sizzle of an old bonfire, but there's no harm in planning for a big blast-off when my spirit separates from my body. There will surely be a liberation from earthly bonds, perhaps like that which John Gillespie Magee celebrates in his poem, "High Flight":

> Oh, I have slipped the surly bonds of Earth
> And danced the skies on laughter-silvered wings; . . .
> The high untrespassed sanctity of space,
> Put out my hand, and touched the face of God.

None of us can peel all the layers off of what life after death will be like. No one can know for sure what happens or how it will be. Some accept death is as a finality and nothing more. Some accept it as the comfort of being united with the elements of earth and contributing to those elements on this planet. Others trust in being welcomed by a loving Presence. However we look upon our death and what lies beyond it, when our time arrives may we be at peace with how we are approaching this awesome transition.

# *Earth Wants Us Back*

*The stars created the atoms of our body.*

~ Brian Swimme

In my sixties I noticed what my elders had sometimes alluded to and what I'd quietly noticed—how they were being drawn toward the ground. What they were describing was how the body loses some of its height as the smooth, elastic cartilage between the joints wears out and the spinal column shrinks due to bone loss. At the same time, shoulders bend forward, breasts grow heavier and droop downward. Even the skin beneath the jawline starts sagging. All the facial creams, pills, and wrinkle-reducing surgeries cannot force the body to live a falsehood forever. We old people are descending downward.

I doubt that any of us pay attention to gravity and how it allows our bodies to remain grounded wherever we go on the planet instead flying off into space. The last decades, however, will remind us often of this scientific reality. As we age, the determined pull of gravity has the last word. The very bones of our bodies give way, weaken, and slowly deteriorate as they give in to this strong magnetism.

One day it occurred to me how natural it is for this process to take place. Earth wants us back. Thanks to the studies of cosmologists like Brian Swimme, we now know that our physical self is composed of the gaseous elements of stars that eventually evolved into the dense material of planets, our Earth being one of them. Here is how spiritual teacher Kabir Helminski conveys the amazing development of our physical being:

> The body is formed by the creative and energizing power of Life out of the substances of this earth. It has arisen out of the lands and seas. . . . It is recycled material. The soul makes use of this body-mind. Through the beneficence of the Source of Life, we can touch, smell, hear, see and feel. . . . We can grasp the beauty and meaning of being lovers on this earth.

It is not just a romantic saying that we are *made of stardust*. We are. And when we Christians hear "Dust thou art and to dust thou shall return" as the dark smudge of Ash Wednesday is placed on our forehead in the shape of a cross, it's like saying "You are from the atoms, the material of Earth, and eventually you're going to return to that home." Perhaps this thought triggers an unpleasant feeling. I find the prospect comforting. I'm happy that Earth wants me back. I'm grateful for how my physical self contains the minerals of our planet, minerals that for so long a time I have been able to enliven and use. What a gift to be on loan for over eighty years.

There's a giant-sized tree by the path where my friend and I go for a walk near her home. I've named this matriarchal cottonwood tree the "Grandmother." She's weather-beaten, with a large strip of bark on the ground beside her trunk. Squirrels nest near the top of her wide-stretching branches. All sorts of insects, mosses, and lichens find a home there. The Grandmother is aging, dying, entering into a final phase, perhaps a long one, maybe not. Eventually she will collapse and slowly blend into the soil as all of creation, including humans, will ultimately do as they join in the cycle of regeneration. This is the natural outcome of any living being. We begin to age when we are born. The process of life, death, and new life occurs for animate and inanimate forms alike. Even stones gradually crumble and mingle with the soil that will eventually bring forth something new.

If ever I am in Rhode Island I will visit the *Roger Williams National Memorial*. His body was originally buried behind his house. Years later, the people of Rhode Island wanted to provide a proper memorial to this founder of their state and had the gravesite excavated. What those who dug there found were "nails, teeth and bone fragments." One other item they uncovered was an amazing apple tree root that "looked as if it had taken on the form of Roger Williams. It had traveled the length of Williams's body, splitting at the hips, bending at the knees and turning up at the feet." What a marvel. That tree obviously fed on the phosphorus in Williams's bones and nurtured the tree's growth.

With this awareness of our co-mingling with the elements of our planet, more people are choosing to be cremated and have their ashes strewn in places that meant a lot to them, including oceans and bubbling mountain streams. Some have decided on a natural burial, which consists of the body being wrapped in a cloth and placed in the ground in that way, instead of being sealed in a thickly-walled coffin.

Others have opted to have their bodies be composted and returned directly to the soil, a metamorphosis of their physical elements that immediately nurtures new life.

Whatever we decide to have done with our physical remains, one thing seems certain: Earth will claim our bodies when we die. She will welcome us back into her darkened womb, draw us in, and take our physical self home. If we find these considerations strange, perhaps even abhorrent, it could be that this is the opportune time to go outside and sit in a park or a flower garden, lean against a tree, or stroll through a cemetery. Do nothing except receive the breath of air, see the colors greeting your eyes, smell the fragrance of flower petals, and touch the bark on a tree.

We are kin to the life around us, which has also been formed from the substance of a planet birthed from the stars. When I stroll outside, I remember that the deceased ones I dearly love who can seem so far from me are intimately near, not only in the soil but also in spirit. We are co-mingled, one with another. I trust that some part of my friends' physicality is with me. I look for this as I walk on the land. I breathe their essence with every intake of air. I sense their presence in the footprints I make along the path. I hold each one in memory, knowing how intertwined we are.

This morning I bring to mind the many who are no longer here. Departed. Left. *Gone*. Rather a strange term—gone. Yes, they have left. But they are with me still, in ways I cannot prove but of which I am keenly aware. I reach to touch the needles on a blue spruce and wonder if a trace of a loved one resides there.

# *This Is Not God's Waiting Room*

*Our development is fueled by the need*
*to adapt to new circumstances.*
*Time passes so quickly that our lives*
*feel as fading as jet contrails.*

~ Mary Pipher

When *National Geographic*'s reporter, Jacqueline Salmon, visited Sun City, Arizona, she discovered how enthusiastic the fifty-five and older residents were. Fifty-five seems like kindergarten compared to the eighties and beyond, but the younger-getting-older people also have to face the awareness of their death drawing closer to them. The strong message in the article indicates that these getting-older persons do not dwell on their mortality, however. They give themselves to a full enjoyment of life.

Hobbies galore and the supportive community of retired persons led one woman to comment, "This is not God's waiting room. Everyone is active and doing something." So what did she mean by that? Is Sun City one big distraction, a continual frenzy of activity so no one has time to think about or acknowledge the possibility of not living forever? Or is it a place that encourages people to enjoy every day to the utmost while they can, knowing life's pleasures are not to be denied to them any more than they are to the youthful? Could Sun City reflect both aspects?

No matter how positively we approach our aging, we are bound to have moments of remembering that time is fleeting and mortality is real. Sometimes these reminders come so close we can almost smell death's breath. Such was the day a few weeks after Christmas when I stopped briefly to drop off a book at a friend's home. She was young, late sixties compared to my almost eighty. Carol was having one of those "my death is real" shudders as she took off the tree-lights and decorations. Although my friend's voice sounded sad and she felt death's possibility, her departure did not show up that year—and still has not—but death's nearness gained momentum as the iron-clad truth intruded upon her tasks.

I didn't think about another dimension of our conversation until later. When Carol and I were conversing about our sense of death being not that far off as we age, I was standing on the threshold of her porch's doorway. I was neither in the living room nor out on the porch. This neither-in-nor-out is like an older person's relationship to mortality. When young, we're far back from the threshold that will carry us to the other side. But in the final decades we stand right there in the doorway, never knowing when the moment of our passing through will arrive.

Continually thinking and talking about dying can keep us from living life here and now. Always letting death poke its nose into our affairs throws us emotionally out of sync. Constantly ruminating about when we, or our loved ones, will die can leave us missing out on the lovely pleasures meant to satisfy us. We need balance—to be intrigued and engaged as much as possible with life's gratuitous opportunities while also keeping an eye on humanity's impermanence and what eventually lies ahead for us.

Deborah McCann reflects on this point in her booklet, *The Gifts of Aging*: "Far from 'waiting to die,' Pope Francis looks on aging and the gift of old age as waiting to *live*. This means using our time to sow seeds of goodness, kindness, tenderness, and wisdom wherever and however we can." Likewise, poet Samantha Reynold cheers on old age in her poem, and refuses to see herself as discarded. Instead, the poet considers herself as "rare," a one-of-a-kind, as "the standing ovation at the end of the play." Reynolds concludes "Walk in Beauty" by insisting she is not "waiting to die." She is "waiting to be found." In other words, she values who she is and refuses to have herself be viewed as a throwaway by society. She's not denying death. Rather, she is celebrating the life she has while she has it, knowing she will eventually leave it behind.

There are elders who feel burdened with living, who keep repeating, "I'm ready; why doesn't God take me?" Actually, it isn't God who's doing the taking. The body has a wisdom and timing of its own. For eighty and more years, elders have told their body *Stay healthy. Fight for life. Hang on. Keep me alive.* And now they're giving the opposite message, *Stop, Quit. I've had enough. I don't want you around anymore. Let me go.* The poor body. So confused.

I once heard an old man, tired of living, say, "I'm useless. Just take me outside and shoot me." If you're like a friend of mine whose body has ceaseless pain, it's understandable to say something like what she said when she remarked, "At age eighty-nine, I'm ready for God to take me home anytime." The same desire existed for a member of my community when mobility complications forced her to move to skilled care in a nursing home. She insisted, "I just want to die." A dread of being in a nursing home led my mother to be more disposed for death. But unlike some persons who focus on waiting, she continued to relish life and was eager to play cards, go to a movie, and share a meal with friends.

Some few people do have the ability to choose to die quickly when this is their wish. Others linger on and on for another decade or more. Try as one might, when we will die remains a puzzle. We humans do not have all the pieces, we do not know the timing, but we do have an option as to how we will regard the ending of our life and how we will live until we die.

The last decades of life ought to not be a stifling waiting room where we just sit and wait for our name to be called. We need to keep adapting to new circumstances. Enjoy what we can while we can. Be enthused with the happiness that comes our way, whether a heart-opening song, a comedy movie, a suspense-filled novel, or a dash of friendship. The underlying question is this: How do we keep our emotional equilibrium between awareness of our future departure and continuing to taste the sweetness of living? We naturally swing between the two as we grow older.

Let's be at peace with the swinging, while choosing to immerse ourselves in the beauty, wonder, and happy surprises coming our way while we are still able to enjoy them.

IX

# Hope and Purpose

## "The Taste of Life and Death"

You reach a point in your life
when you ask if loss is going to
barge in unceasingly.

You barely recover from one sorrow
and another beats upon your door.
When some brief respite of relief
returns, you quietly hold your breath
and wait for the next unwanted incident
to come stomping in.

You have a sense that life will
always have the taste of death
from now on. Your own age
pushes you to ponder the inevitable.
You wonder if life will ever again
be untouched by what brings pain.

Age, sickness, accidents, deaths—
you've had enough of this suffering.
You think it wouldn't hurt so much
but it still has the same swollen feet.

Just about the time you are sure
you'll drown in constant endings
and be devoured by the hungry
mouth of heartache and farewells,
along comes a simple happening
to discount your depressing theory.

A grandchild is born, a friendship
enters, a stubborn illness departs,
nature reveals surprising beauty;
you find enough joyful revelations
for hope to take a reviving breath
in your aging, battered heart.

~ Joyce Rupp

# *Sustaining Our Hope*

*When my grandson Brandon was four and a half,*
*I asked him if he ever had a bad day.*
*"No," he said. "Never?," I asked.*
*He thought a bit and then said,*
*"Yeah, but it ended good."*

~ Rivvy Neshama

One of my favorite walks goes around the spacious Red Feather Prairie, bordered by Saylorville Lake and woodlands. When autumn arrives, my spirit thrills with the beauty of the prairie. Tall compass flowers of brilliant yellow border both sides of the path. Across the meadow tanned prairie grasses with purple hues reach above my head and wave languorously in the wind. Imagine my dismay in late September when I arrived to see nothing in that vast expanse of flowers and high grasses, nothing except charred earth and the barely visible nubs of decimated plants.

The park rangers had burned the native grasses for the first time since I began walking there several years ago. I knew intellectually that this action was meant to nourish and restore lush growth in the coming year, but emotionally

I detested the look of the brutally shorn land. Imagine, then, my wild joy the following spring when I detected tiny green shoots springing up on the midst of that bleakness. By mid-summer the grasses and compass plants were well on their way, and by the time autumn arrived their grandeur sang in my heart.

As I stood gazing at the prairie's restored life, it occurred to me that the process of the prairie's being razed completely and then restored demonstrated the seemingly impossible becoming possible. I thought of how a similar process happens in the human heart when we are shorn and seared of our flourishing contentment. At my age, what did I anticipate might happen as a result of the inherent losses bound to scorch my inner landscape? Did I believe in a future "greening" even if what currently gave joy was seared to the nub? I was aware that I could not regain the infinite energy of childhood nor the productive vigor of earlier adulthood. My body could not regain its suppleness, nor reclaim a keener memory. Neither would I be able to bring back cherished people who had passed on.

Accepting these realities, I considered what sustains my hope: appreciating and enjoying life, maintaining valuable relationships and being open to new ones, and savoring going slower—which allows for greater attentiveness to my inner life, discovering more of who I truly am. I'm confident hope will persist and bring forth newness if I linger longer with the joy I find in nature, reading, music, and art, while being faithful to daily reflection.

In scripture, the virtue of hope is symbolized as a ship's anchor. (Hebrews 6:19) An anchored boat holds steady in a stormy sea, just as our hope can keep us grounded when life wants to twirl us around and destroy our confidence. Hope tells us our spirit can hold together when life as we have known it disintegrates.

I was especially grateful to come across the following hope-filled biblical story telling of the prophet Elijah's experience of depression. He's fleeing from his enemies and has lost hope that his society will change. His situation reflects the spirit of people today whose suffering bears down on them so intensely that they lose confidence, believing, like Elijah, that death would be easier than remaining in their current situation.

> But he himself went a day's journey into the wilderness, and came and sat down under a solitary broom tree. He asked that he might die: "It is enough; now, O Lord, take away my life. . . ." Then he lay down under the broom tree and fell asleep. Suddenly an angel touched him and said to him "Get up and eat." He looked, and there at his head was a cake baked on hot stones, and a jar of water. (1Kings 19:6)

I wrote the following in my journal after marveling at this unknown presence who "touched him," bringing Elijah food and drink to sustain his life, encouraging him to go forth with restored strength for the journey:

> Who are the unknown angels, the nameless,
> faceless ones, who come to us unsought,
> arriving to ease our agonizing journey
> through the desert of lost hope and dashed joy?

What are the hearth cakes, the jugs of water,
left there to revive our desolate spirit—
those brief encounters that only later on
we recognize as the balm they've been for us?

These angels travel not with silver wings
but with compassionate, human hearts,
moved by a guided nudge from inside
to speak a word, leave a smile, send a message.

They gift us with restored hope and purpose
to carry us through another day of desert,
perhaps far beyond that one precious deed,
moving us into freedom from what spiraled us
downward when we thought all was lost.

As Kate DiCamillo professes in *Louisiana's Way Home*, "And perhaps what matters when all is said and done is not who puts us down but who picks us up."

Who are the "angels" who've come along in your time of need and picked you up? How has your hope been restored?

# *Ache for Your Life*

*There are wild flowers in my desert*
*which take up to twenty years to bloom.*
*The seeds sleep like geodes beneath hot feldspar sand*
*until a flash flood bolts the arroyo, lifting them*
*in its copper current, opens them with memory—*
*they remember what their god whispered*
*into their ribs: wake up and ache for your life.*

~ Natalie Diaz

Natalie Diaz's poem leads me to ask: What might the wild flowers be that sleep in the arroyos of my inner world? Am I aching for them to come alive? Will my aging process contribute to this awakening? What will it take for that process to proceed? All of this is like asking "Am I hopeful there is still more beauty, goodness, and delight to resurrect in my life?" As I enter my eighth decade, I respond positively to that last question.

Hope for what? That the sleeping seeds of my inner self may serve as sources for good no matter how frail I might become; that life will bring about a sense of well-being; that I am able to express love for the people in my life; that my offering of compassion can yield the gift of easing the suffering of others; that I may be willing to notice the sources of joy that are everywhere. I'm aware that my personal development still has more seeds to awaken, that fuller meaning and transformative perceptions await in my becoming a cognizant elder. I trust my small deeds, good intentions, and positive gestures to make a difference in our ailing world.

I have hope of these things because I know more and more women and men in their late years who are giving themselves as fully as they can to be relevant, caring human beings. A lot of "wild flowers" have blossomed. My relatives, friends, colleagues, and acquaintances participate in daily activities with whole-hearted interest. They engage in volunteer work of all sorts, assist underserved students and help with immigrant resettlement, work at food pantries and homeless shelters. They attend book clubs, political rallies, poetry groups, and faithfully go to the gym. Many are active in their church or local communities.

Elders who have reasonably good health continue being active. Others not so fortunate spend considerable time at medical appointments. Some older persons are limited by physical disabilities, while others experience few maladies. Each of them does the best they can to continue to activate the dormant seeds of love within themselves. Some elders offer the best of gifts by allowing others to care for them when they cannot care for themselves.

Contrary to general opinion in Western society, the later years of life can be a time of pleasure and general contentment. Older persons still contribute significantly to the well-being of society. Hope-filled elders of an increasing population are not moaning, complaining, or whining about "being old." At the same time, they are honest about the gradual decline inherent in every living creature. Elders recognize that each human life eventually reaches a final conclusion. Until that time arrives, they delight in life, maintain a vibrant hope, and celebrate the gift of their existence with gratitude.

John O'Donohue cautions, "Old age, like illness, is a time when you really need to mind yourself. If you get hooked on some of the downward pulls of gravity in your soul, it can be a time of torture so that you pray for release —to die would be total peace." After giving that advice, O'Donohue then proceeds to encourage having hope in spite of what is difficult: "If you look on it as a time of possibility, amazing things can happen. A good axiom in life is to try to see the possibilities in a situation. Often in a situation, it is the walls we see, and we never see the windows of possibilities and the places where thoughts and feelings can grow."

A good portion of society sees in the stage of Elderhood a downturn, a long series of disintegrations. This view constitutes only one side (and often not a side at all) of how the later years evolve. Consider my older sister and brother-in-law. A lot of dormant seeds are being birthed in their eighties. At their current ages of eighty-three and eighty-seven, he suffers from kidney failure. A year ago he was hospitalized for two weeks, suffering from a life-threatening infection. My sister contends with hands crippled by arthritis, along with insistent back and neck pain. They both wear hearing aids. Yet these things do not keep them from participating in life with incredible gusto. They cheer on their favorite football teams, discover new restaurants, attend jazz festivals and numerous events involving their great-grandchildren. They have a community of friends in their social life and in their church. I never hear them complain of constraints or illnesses. They welcome and fit in as much daily activity as is doable.

Harsh realities of "growing old" exist, but older age also provides sources of positiveness. Yes, there is a downside to the final years, but is any stage of life all roses and no thorns? Of course not. Each life consists of smooth terrain and bumpy paths. In her usual good humor, Anne Lamott in *Almost Everything* approaches aging with a hopeful voice:

> Hope changes as you get a little older, from the hope that this or that happens, to hope in life, old friends, laughter, art, goodness, helpers. I hope and am amazed, some early mornings, at just finding myself alive. I thought as I approached eighteen years old that I was a goner for sure. And here I am, still alive, still here, and often in a good mood. Other early mornings? Not so much. My back aches, my vision fades, I can't concentrate. It's like the Samuel Beckett novel—"you must go on, I can't go on, I'll go on."

Perhaps some older persons would agree with Jane Hirshfield that

> hope is the hardest
> love we carry.

In my experience of aging, I would rewrite those two lines: "Hope is the most *resilient* love we carry." However it is that we view hope, may it steady our spirit and help us to ache for our lives "like trees planted by streams of water, which yield their fruit in its season" (Psalm 1:3, 4).

# *Find Joy in the Smallest Things*

*I'm finding the simplest way to happiness*
*is to let myself be happy*
*with the things that make me happy.*

~ Brian Andreas

Some time ago I came across a greeting card with the message "*Find joy in the smallest things.*" This counsel certainly applies to older people. Big booming joys show up less, but a lot of smaller joys filter through the days just waiting for us to greet them. I used to expect happiness to be high waterfalls and robust ocean waves. As I've aged, I find my joy in simple things like tiny Jordan Creek. I like to stand and listen to the sound of the shallow water gurgling over a patch of stones in summer or pressing forward under winter's snow.

Joy is a vitamin for hope. Simple pleasures can prevent us from teetering into boredom or becoming dispirited. Sources of enjoyment beckon us to enter into the pleasing parts of the day. My eighty-nine-year-old friend finds some of her best moments sitting and observing a forty-foot-tall scotch pine tree by the window of her bedroom. Jane has watched that tree span outward and upward for more than twenty-five years. As the tree grew, she grew in the habit of observation. What joy she's found in birds peering out from where they've made a home, watching the green nibs of pine cones mature through the summer, seeing raindrops sparkle at the ends of needles and fluffy snowflakes pile up on the branches.

Not long ago, Sister Zita at age ninety-four enthusiastically described how much she appreciates color, "There's red and then there's *red*. So many shades." Our conversation reminded me of a book that awakened my attentiveness to the smallest things when I was in my forties. In Frederick Franck's *The Zen of Seeing/Drawing*, he invites workshop participants to go outside with him, to find a spot in nature where he asks them to sit down. Then, Franck encourages them to really behold what they are seeing: "Let your eyes fall on whatever happens to be in front of you. It may be a plant or a bush or a tree, or perhaps just some grass. Then close your eyes for the next five minutes."

Then Franck asks the group to open their eyes and instructs them to focus on what they observe:

> "Look it in the eye, until you feel it looking back at you. Feel that you are alone with it on Earth! That it is the most important thing in the universe, that it contains all the riddles of life and death. It does! You are no longer looking. You are seeing." After this activity, a participant confided to Franck, "I am a widow and live alone, and I often feel lonely. Today I learned that if you really see the things around you, you're not lonely anymore."

Contrary to the axiom "You can't teach an old dog new tricks," we are never too old to develop a fresh, attitude-altering habit. Why not begin to use the gift of our physical senses to find joy? If our eyesight has grown dim, our hearing can take pleasure in human voices, birdsongs, and favorite music. If hearing fails us, we might focus on feeling the touch of another person's hand in ours, a soft breeze on our face, the flow of warm water on our skin. If our ability to taste isn't what it once was, we can still appreciate the texture, color, and shape of the food we consume. There's always something at which we can marvel and be joyful about if we are intentional about observing life closely.

Not long ago I was out for a walk by the river when an older couple ambled by the shoreline, obviously arguing about who was going to hold the leash of their thick-muscled boxer. When the man grabbed the leash from the woman, she frowned at him and muttered something inaudible. Watching and hearing that encounter reminded me that sometimes old age mellows and sometimes it disgruntles. In the latter case, there's little happiness to be found. The joy exists, but it's misted over with a cloud of annoyances.

How did that couple end up that way? Were they always dissatisfied, or did this disposition gradually claim their personality and stifle their delight in life? Or was this simply an exceptionally grouchy day for one of them? I don't know, but it revived my intention to not slip into a negative mode in my old age. Young people have such a short history and long road ahead while we oldsters have a lot of story and life experience to dig around in and savor. The road ahead of us is short, but the one we are on has plenty for us to feast on if we are willing to seek joy without expecting it to arrive in large doses.

Some older persons grow stodgy and set in their ways, deciding there's no more adventure or learning to be had. Others choose to enter into their aging process with an open mind and heart, stretching and growing. As a friend of mine quipped: "We have a choice in how we respond. We always have a choice." I would add: We have a choice in *how* we respond to what is happening to us, but we do not always have a choice in *what* is actually happening. If the choice we make includes the *Zen of seeing*, we will more likely find opportunities for hope and happiness.

I learned a hard lesson about this in my late seventies. A longtime friend and I enjoyed years of visits and travel. I presumed we would grow old together. So did she. Someplace in my rational mind I knew we would each die. Occasionally I wondered which of us would "go first." But I presumed we still had good years remaining. In early November she decided we wouldn't get together as we had planned for later that month (we lived four hundred miles apart). She said, "Let's wait until next spring." But that get-together "next spring" never happened. A brain tumor discovered soon after that decision took her life a few months later.

I encourage every elder: *Do not put off what you hope to say or to do with one another; give yourself fully to what you want to enjoy in the remaining years that you have left.*

# *Having a Purpose*

*Finding our purpose is what guides us and gives our life meaning.*

~ Jo Ann Jenkins

Jann Freed asks, "If you are what you do and you don't do it anymore, then who are you?" This author and leadership coach suggests that everyone needs a purpose: "Your reason for getting up in the morning can be called your purpose." As we grow into the late years, finding that purpose can be more challenging, especially if health is declining and physical mobility becomes impaired.

For elders who retain an ability to be mobile and whose energy allows them to use their talents in a more active manner, purpose in life helps build a sense of self-worth and provides the assurance of still having something of value to be shared. Frank Cunningham acknowledges this in *Vesper Time*:

> Gone is the regimentation and responsibility of the workplace. Most of us are glad to put those aspects of work behind us. But also gone is the purpose that was rooted in mission and commitment. And without purpose, we drift into malaise.

I remember a pastor who, worn out from overwork in his parish, was eagerly looking forward to his forthcoming retirement. When I met him at a gathering a year later, I inquired how he was enjoying his long-sought freedom. He blurted out, "I need something to do!" He went on to explain how bored he felt "doing nothing." With retirement, he lost a meaningful purpose for his life and knew he had to find something to restore it.

How do we reach beyond ourselves, nudge our resilient self to have a reason to wake up each day when we're "feeling our age" or besieged by unmitigated pain? What might motivate us to uncover meaning and satisfaction? Some aging persons cannot leave their residence without assistance, and some struggle with illness. For certain elders it takes most of the day to care for self by getting dressed, taking medicine, bathing, eating, and sleeping. In such circumstances questions like "Why am I still living?" might arise. Is it possible for all of us to have a purpose, no matter how old, healthy or unhealthy, we are?

What might someone with weakened, arthritic hands or congestive heart failure count as purposeful? It's easy to forget that even the smallest of things makes a difference. In *God Never Blinks*, Regina Brett tells how her aging uncle, whose life held a lot sorrow and illness, reached beyond himself and gave her a gift she still keeps close by: "My uncle called one random day just to tell me how proud he is of me. I saved the message and replay it to hear his voice, shaky from Parkinson's and age, still full of sweet gratitude."

The later years of life do not have to end up as a tedious existence. It does not take long to meet older men and women avoiding this dullness by engaging in activities that contribute to something worthwhile. Here are some whom I've met in person or in printed resources, all in their late eighties or mid-nineties: Imelda, creating greeting cards on her computer; Jill, expressing joy at folding a basketful of her great grandchildren's newly washed clothes; Alan, buying a sewing machine after treatments for colon cancer and now creating stunning purses; Marlys, serving on the library board at a senior residence; Ginger, learning to quilt; Bill, actively supporting candidates for political office; and Vera, after healing from a broken hip, still playing the organ each week at her church. Each of us can do something purposeful, even when we experience physical limitations, like England's Captain Tom Moore. When he was in his late nineties he raised almost thirty million pounds for charity by walking laps around his garden with his walker during the Covid-19 epidemic.

I came upon one of the most precious scenes of an older person with a reason to wake up each day when I found ninety-three year old Sister Rosalie taking care of her friend's parakeet. As I watched this tiny woman wearing oversized yellow gloves dip into a basin of water to clean the birdcage, she described as best she could with her stroke-impaired speech how she had become fond of this unassuming act of kindness. What joy her modest and deliberate deed elicited. It reminded me that no matter how old we are, we can find a reason to go on with our life, one that assures us we still have something to give.

For older people who are ill and frail, having a purpose does not proceed from big actions, but in the slow, patient movement of both body and spirit in being thoughtful and kind to one's self and others. With increasing physical diminishment, our purpose in life might be that of taking care of ourselves. Can we be satisfied if our aging moves us to the state of ministering to our own self as lovingly as we would to another infirm person? Our goal might consist of putting on socks and shoes for another day without feeling irritated about this activity taking thirty minutes.

Perhaps one of the most overlooked gestures in having purpose and meaning for both giver and receiver is that of prayer. Long ago I met Marie whose physical self was becoming increasingly limited. She confided that her central work in late life was visualizing herself walking along an ocean shoreline where she daily named each of her children and grandchildren, placing them in God's hands. The value she found in this purpose is noted in *Give Us This Day,* in which Robert Ellsberg quotes Robert Lax, poet and contemplative:

> Prayer is a way of doing instantaneous good for all things in all places. It's a way of sending out love everywhere at once. . . . Prayer makes everything you do more real, lasting, meaningful, and fruitful. Through prayer, everything just flowers and flows.

It takes so little to make a difference in how someone goes through a day. A smile, a thank you, or a genuine compliment can lift a heart and send a person on their way feeling better about themselves. Each of us can find a purpose out of which we live. We trust that a loving message of care, or a prayer quietly sent from our heart, has worth for the life of another.

X

# Identity

*I have to let go of the person I was*
*and accept the person I now am.*

*~ Terese Lux*

## "Let Go of the Person I Was"

Let go of the one totally in charge,
the one who had no fear of falling,
of breaking an ankle, a leg, an arm,
or worse—suffer a brain bleed.

Let go of the one skilled at doing,
being successful and productive,
confident and self-possessed,
able to handle most everything.

Let go of the person whose alert brain
easily recalled a name, a description,

details of a story lodged in the past,
and where a precious item was placed.

Let go of having a healthy, active body
ready to obey and serve each command.
Let go of energy once quick and plentiful,
rarely collapsing with utter weariness.

Greet this unwanted stranger's arrival,
waiting to receive a respectful welcome.
Get to know and accept her new traits;
do not shun, deny, reject or criticize.

Rather, behold with a gaze of kindness
this one still looking over her shoulder
longing to be the woman she once was.
Learn to love and appreciate her now

for she still bears the same loving spirit,
still intends to live with zestful gratitude,
still cherishes what is of utmost value,
still retains a home in Eternity's Heart.

~ Joyce Rupp

# *Meeting Mystery in Old Age*

*Where are the roots of our being?*
*They plunge back and down into the unfathomable past.*
*How great is the mystery of the first cells*
*which were one day animated by the breath of our souls.*

~ Pierre Teilhard de Chardin

Ever since I was quite young I have searched my interior landscape for "the meaning of life." The endless pieces and layers that comprise my self often intrigue me. I marvel at how such pieces and layers form the substance of each human being as we develop. What constitutes a person and how do they get to be who they are? Such a big question, one that follows us into Elderhood and pokes at us to get our attention.

We often meet mystery when we consider the many fragments that shape our existence, the beliefs and viewpoints that take hold and direct us as we mature. These principles and values fashion the framework of our personhood. In late life, if we are willing to explore the wonderment of who we are and what we believe, we can gain a sense of what our life has meant and how to embrace it.

What life-principles have you counted on for your integrity? Which ones continue to be relevant as your future years shrink in number? Do some of your beliefs and attitudes require examination? What grounds your love and sustains your faith? How does this influence your living?

When I peer into these questions for myself at my age, I notice how differently I view many of the things I once believed about divinity and structured religion. The God of my youth no longer looks upon me as unworthy and having to "shape up." Now I relate to a Great Love moving through the universe in ways I cannot explain yet choose to accept with my whole heart. While I continue to be connected to my religious tradition, I no longer feel compelled and confined by its compulsory dictates if they no longer reflect the teachings and spirit of Jesus.

When we think about our personal identity, we may discover that some of our questions do not have answers—and we slowly accept this unsolvable reality. Gerald May came to this conclusion after a long and painful period of depression and treatment for cancer. In *The Dark Night of the Soul*, May wrote:

> It is a slow and sometimes painful process of becoming "as little children" again, in which we make friends with mystery and finally fall in love again with it. And in that love we find an ever increasing freedom to be who we really are in an identity that is continually emerging and never defined. We are freed to join the dance of life in fullness without having a clue about what the steps are.

Last year my journey into personal identity and the accompanying mystery found affirmation in a touching story Fr. Paddy Gilger related in *Give Us This Day*. He described his seminary professor, an erudite biblical scholar who could write "the word 'spirit' in ten languages, from memory." One day Gilger approached this man to seek an answer to his confusion about a biblical verse related to the resurrection of Jesus. Gilger asked his teacher if he believed the story. After considerable silence the man responded, "I don't know." A bit later he added, "I don't know, but something happened. How else did those men go from cowering in fear to going willingly to their deaths? I don't know what, but something happened that made them free." Gilger then muses: "His tone was that of an aging man of immense learning who'd found that a lifetime of effort to ground his faith in knowledge had thrown him back into the abyss of faith."

Being "thrown back into the abyss of faith" is what growing old can do to us. Experiencing mystery is not a "bad thing" to have happen. The honest reply to Paddy Gilger's question joins us with other elders who may be moving away from what were considered to be precise truths. We become comfortable with the mellow mistiness of the unknown and unresolved, and decide to be at peace with that unknowing.

Pondering what one believes and coming to fresh conclusions is not unusual for older people, but we might not speak of this for fear we are alone on this journey of questioning and searching for clarity about identity and meaning. Like other searching seniors, we do not want to be judged as "negative" or 'faith-less." We ought not fear this process of exploration but welcome it as a way of coming to greater tranquility. Having a wise person be a companion to us on this investigative journey helps greatly, whether this be a trusted peer or a skilled professional.

With guidance on our spiritual path we have fewer stumbles and less chance of falling into the potholes of angst that might unexpectedly appear.

As I investigate meaning in late life, I have a vivid memory of my sister-in-law's sewing room where big sacks hold hundreds of small remnants left over from the beautiful quilts she's created. When I took one of those sacks to my cousin Abbey's young children, they immediately emptied the colorful remnants in the sack on to the living room floor where they wow-ed, laughed, and enjoyed sorting the colors and shapes into new patterns for themselves. Our lives contain their own sack of remnants, among which we search for what holds enough content to form new patterns for living in the stage of Elderhood.

Jungian psychologist Jane R. Prétat suggests: "To accept ourselves and our lives as they are is a lesson we would all like to learn." This is surely the result of what Job experienced as he questioned the meaning of his existence after a multitude of disasters rained down on him. The simple statement of 42:17 in the *Book of Job,* "And Job died, old and full of days," tells us nothing of the layers of his journey unless we have read about those years in the book's early chapters. They are filled with success and failure, consolation and desolation, struggle and acquiescence.

Job ended his life in peace, but not before he examined his assumptions about life. Only then could he calmly surrender to mystery and give a humble bow.

# *Who Am I Now?*

*I have walked through many lives,*
*some of them my own,*
*and I am not who I was,*
*though some principle of being*
*abides, from which I struggle*
*not to stray.*

~ Stanley Kunitz

When I wrote the poem, "Old Maps No Longer Work" in *Dear Heart, Come Home*, I thought I was one of the few who felt that way. I soon discovered that being unsure about who I was and how the years would progress was something that resonated with a lot of readers, especially this verse:

> no map, no specific directions,
> no "this way ahead" or "take a left"
> how will I know where to go?

*How will I find my way? No map!* That poem surfaced in me at age fifty. Now in my early eighties, I find much of it ringing true again. I'm learning, as I did with midlife readers, that I am not alone in this wondering and wandering as I step into old age. Others in Elderhood also question and examine who they are.

Many workers when they reach retirement age eagerly anticipate the freedom it promises. But once regularly scheduled work ends and its wearisome cloak falls away, questions surface about how to maintain cherished self-identity, how to occupy one's time, and how to leave behind what may have fed their false notion of who they were. In their sixties and seventies people still have many activities in which they can engage, but in the years stretching out after that, a larger set of deeply seated wonderings emerges. These big questions dig deeply and uproot how we have identified ourselves by what shaped our lives.

*Who am I . . .*

If I have a limited amount of energy?

If I can't remember nearly as well as I used to?

If I am less healthy than in the past?

If I lose my ability to see or hear?

If most of my close friends die before I do?

If I can no longer drive a car?

If I develop incontinence?

If my judgment is increasingly impaired?

If I move away from my much-loved home?

If I have to rely on a walker or wheelchair for mobility?

If I have the whole day before me and nothing to do?

If I am now a single person after decades of marriage?

If I am rarely appreciated or affirmed?

If I can't find a meaningful purpose to my life?

If there's never a day without physical pain?

In *Coming to Age* Jane Prétat reminds her readers that in each stage of life, personal growth requires that we redefine ourselves. She knows it's a difficult task to leave behind the former self, to lose the security of past identity and wait until a new one emerges:

> When we find ourselves in a liminal time/space vestibule between one way of being and another, our conscious energy is apt to disappear into the unconscious and become unavailable to us in our daily life. It is as if we fell asleep on the road to age. When this happens, we may feel as if we've suddenly lost pieces of ourselves. Our persona, the way we "clothe" ourselves in public, may become damaged. Then we are unfamiliar even to our instinctual selves. . . . We feel out of sorts, wondering who we have become.

Not long ago I listened to a woman widowed a year earlier after a long and happy marriage. As Jill reflected, she commented, "Only when my life partner died did I feel old. I'm slowly feeling more like myself again and knowing who I am now. I'm learning to live with the new me." At age eighty-six, Jill knew that only by "going within" would she establish her true identity.

When Scottish Dougie McLean sings in "Rescue Me," "*On this mountain's the only place I can see clearly,*" something strong stands up inside of me and reaches for this kind of inner clarity. It is a longing for lucidity about identity. As

I make the final laps around the track of life, I want to see and lean into how to live the best of who I am, to be an authentic, loving human being, and to contribute by easing the aching of this world.

I do not recall a time when I was scared to search within myself, but I have known people who, when faced with the possibility of searching, run the other way. They've confided fears such as, *It's a waste of time. I won't find anything. I'm afraid of what I'll find. I could get lost in there. It's just being self-centered to do that.* In my years of accompanying brave people through spiritual guidance, what actually happens when wading through the densely forested parts of our inner being is that eventually we come to an open space where there's a transparent pool. We look into it and see with wonder a person we hardly recognize, someone we want to know and love. This *knowing* takes us homeward to our beauty-full self, allows us to go forward with much more confidence to meet whatever besets us in the future.

As we become the older generation, we learn to accept ourselves, even if we never come up with adequate responses to questions relating to our identity. As we ponder who we are in our final years, some lines from *The Essential Rumi* offer assurance. Even this intuitive, discerning poet did not fully know himself, but he trusted where he came from and where he anticipated arriving. This was enough for him:

> All day I think about it, then at night I say it.
> Where did I come from, and what am I supposed
> to be doing?
> I have no idea.
> My soul is from elsewhere, I'm sure of that,
> and I intend to end up there.

# *Cognitive Impairment*

*A shaft of insight can enter the back of my mind and when I turn to greet it, it is gone.*

~ Florida Scott-Maxwell

The possibility of some form of cognitive impairment affecting us or a loved one can easily hound us in old age. If you have heard yourself saying *I can't remember if... I neglected to tell you.... Stop me if I said this already.... I forgot to mention...*, you are among other elders who do not always have immediate access to everything they want to say. Let a young person forget a name or misplace something and nothing's thought of it. Let this happen to an older person and the red flag of neurological decline starts to frantically wave.

I can surely identify with searching for a word or another piece of information that eludes me. In my younger years, every book title and author were right there on my lips as soon as I wanted to mention them to workshop participants. But gradually, this recall has not been so quick. Now I write notes about notes. And I look each morning on my calendar to be sure I do not miss an appointment or a special event.

For the most part this does not cause me distress. Something a technology person off-handedly mentioned while working on my old, ready-to-conk-out computer gives me comfort and patience when I'm waiting for the longed-for names or stories to appear on my mental screen. In telling me that I needed a new hard drive where the many files were stored, he said something like, "The ridges on the hard drive eventually wear smooth. This slows down the search engine and it is harder to find what's there." I've often thought about this when I'm trying to catch something lodged in my brain and it's nowhere to be found. I don't worry about it (at least, not much). I just wait, like an old computer's hard drive chugging longer to sort through and find where the file is stored.

A weakening of one's memory is as natural as an ankle bone or an inner organ losing some fitness. If my physical balance becomes more unreliable, why wouldn't my brain also experience some lessening of ability? Not every occurrence of anxiety or moment of forgetfulness indicates we're headed toward severe memory loss. While memory lapses are often due to ordinary aging, for some persons changes in the brain can lead to more serious outcomes. Daily details do not only hide out for a while; they become lost forever. Emotional changes that naturally develop with aging accelerate, and they change an older person into someone totally different from the person they were before.

I've found it distressful to watch cognitive impairment in a colleague with whom I'd teamed on a number of retreats. She developed an inability to make adequate connections and appropriate judgments. These changes advanced until her children chose to move their mother to the West Coast, where she could reside in a memory care residence close to them. The best part of me wanted this for my friend because I knew that as she became even further lost from current reality, she would have the love and immediate presence of her children. But I yearned to have the person I loved remain as she once was.

An older person can also be in denial about not being able to function adequately. When our forgetfulness increases significantly, when we become easily disoriented, it's time for medical assistance. You might notice that I am not using the word "dementia" in reference to cognitive decline. I'm indebted to a Canadian correspondent who described the implications of using this word.

> I am accompanying my husband of forty-five years. a brilliant man, educator and leader. On the day of his diagnosis of *Alzheimer's dementia,* he looked at the neurologist, pointed his finger at him, and said: "I am not demented!" My husband who taught Latin and Greek knew the etymology and he wanted to be sure that the neurologist understood that he was not, "out of his mind." The word "dementia" is archaic, and socially stigmatizing. I'm doing what I can here in my circle to help family and friends and medical personnel to consider this and to choose other nomenclature that supports the dignity of the person.

However the neurological changes occur, the essence of the person we love remains. I've learned how graciously and lovingly certain men and women have accompanied parents, spouses, and others close to their heart by living out of this truth. I discovered it again when I wrote about my colleague with memory loss and received this note from Mike who had read my newsletter: "The good-byes you described are becoming so common. I lost my mom to Alzheimer's after an eleven and a half year battle. She taught us so much in her life but she saved the best for last—every encounter was so special."

The details of our lived journey may gradually slide from view, but the treasured essence of our inner being will remain. We are more than what we remember, more than what we forget, more than the personality that developed as our lives progressed. Within us resides a silent communion with love grown and gathered through our years, spun into golden, unbreakable threads. We never lose our essential goodness and the beauty present from when we came forth from the womb. The person we were, the person we knew, may go into hiding, but the core of our personhood remains true, full of light.

We may lose our capability to decipher details and dates, perhaps eventually be unable to communicate in our usual way. People we've long known will visit and we will not recognize them. Maybe none of this will happen to us, but possibly to another person who long ago captured our heart. In either case, inside someone with cognitive impairment lives the endearing person who took a first breath.

# *A Time to Rewild*

*"Alexander Rostov, could it be that you have become settled in your ways?"*

~ Amor Towles

When I see a lively, untamed animal moving across the prairie or if I come across a patch of blazing star flowers dancing in the breeze near a little creek, my heart leaps with joy in knowing they are thriving in a hospitable place. I think of something similar with older people who feel at home and are thriving in being their authentic selves. I agree with John O'Donohue's quip, "It is so invigorating to meet a wild old person who has remained faithful to their wild life force."

It is this "wild life force" on which Florida Scott Maxwell muses:

> My seventies were interesting, and fairly serene, but my eighties are passionate. I grow more intense as I age. . . . Though drab outside—wreckage to the eye. . . . Inside we flame with a wild life that is almost incommunicable. It has to be accepted as passionate life, perhaps the life I never lived, never guessed I had it in me to live. . . . It is a place of fierce energy.

Rather, than implying "out of control," the first definition of the word "wild" conveyed in Webster's dictionary is that of living in a place where one belongs, a natural habitat, an area where life has the best chance to flourish. How many of us in the later years can attest to being that much at home with ourselves—living out of an identity and life force that enables us to flourish in our state of being? A lot of us are probably still trying to recognize and activate that wildness, the home of our authenticity, for this tends to be a life-long process.

For environmentalists, the term "rewild" refers to the effort of letting nature live where it can prosper, doing so by "returning an area to its natural, wild state," restoring lost lands where forests were overharvested, wetlands drained, and meadows bulldozed for housing developments. The goal is to reestablish the vegetation that naturally grows in those places in order to have more biodiverse habitats where growth easily occurs.

The term "rewild" is also used for humans in their effort to establish a more viable and true connection to the outdoors and simple living. I'm applying it to our eldering years because this stage of life invites us to return to the home of our clearest, staunchest self, to regain the uncluttered genuineness of our early life before we became swamped by societal opinions convincing us we ought to be other than who we truly are. James Birren, director of the UCLA Center on Aging, unknowingly referred to this rewilding when he noted, "Over the years, whenever I asked older students what, if any, regrets they had, one theme emerged: looking back, they wished they had taken more chances to be themselves. They thought their greatest obstacle was their own nature and the limitations they themselves created." Our elders years offer us a last chance to welcome ourselves home. Now is the time to be and to live—not as the culture or our inner, bossy voice dictates—but as the person inside who has been waiting to be known and rebirthed.

I had not been familiar with the term "rewild" until it happened to my mother in her eighth decade, when I observed with amazement how a part of her hidden self changed, how she explored and accepted the home within herself that awaited her return. This woman, who had lived mainly as "a farmer's wife" for almost fifty years, developed an appreciation for theater, explored new ways to pray, enthusiastically traveled on "mystery tours" that introduced her to new vistas, met a new friend who recognized the unlived wildness in my mother and cheered her on.

In *Wild Mercy*, Mirabai Starr reminds her readers, "When you were a child, you knew yourself to be cocreator of the universe. But little by little you forgot who you were. . . . you are forgetting how to move to the music of your soul." That may be the most accurate way to describe rewilding, learning to move to the music of our soul. Mythologist Joseph Campbell described something like this when Bill Moyers interviewed him: "I think that what we're seeking is an experience of being alive, so that our life experiences on the purely physical plane will have resonances within our own innermost being and reality." Recently I became reacquainted with a woman who had been at a retreat with me long ago. In describing what her eighties were like, Mary wrote: "My spirit remains young. The body is another matter. I miss my youthful energy. But filling my life with love and ideas and reflecting on blessings brings me joy and makes my heart smile." Mary is obviously rewilding. Her happiness is the result. George Valliant also mentioned this quality of the heart in a study on aging led by Rabbi Rachel Cowan and Dr. Linda Thal: "I think it enormously important to the next generation that we be happy into old age—and confident—not necessarily that we are right but that it is wonderful to persist in our search for meaning and rectitude. Ultimately, that is our most valuable legacy—the conviction that life is and has been worthwhile right up to the limit."

Older persons who are rewilding evince more peace, smile more easily, and refuse to get caught in the useless details and anxieties that plague their peers. In rewilding, they've chosen to relish aging with a spirit of gladness, discarding concerns about how others see them or expect them to respond. Elders who grow in tune with what is genuine within themselves do not pretend to be other than who they have re-found themselves to be—an authentic human being. This does not indicate a lack of boundaries or a carefreeness that steps on the dignity and rights of others. Rather, the aliveness, the wisdom, and the playfulness in these elders' eyes and voices naturally extends an invitation to those around them to let go of worries over what they cannot control and to find enjoyment in the midst of what weighs them down.

More elders are casting aside their "should" and "ought" in order to release their wildness. They're shaking loose the tight strictures caging their personalities and steadily opening to what this amazing world holds for their appreciation. The bodies of these elders may falter, memories not be what they were, but this does not halt a desire to live from the root of their most honest and freed self. Unafraid to be who they are, rewilding elders live as people coming come home to the music of life within themselves.

XI

# Spiritual Transformation

*Yes, all my illusions will burn into*
*illumination of joy, and all my desires*
*ripen into fruits of love.*

~ Rabindranath Tagore

## "Burning My Illusions"

My illusions, oh, they have been many:
the over-used narrative of who I am,
judgments of what to say and when,
false creeds impelling my actions.

Timeworn desires, these, too, abound,
sometimes troublesome and unbearable,
the useless expectations, deceptive hopes
wooing and wrecking my emotional space.

Am I willing to release these misperceptions,
toss them into the purifying pyre of peace,

allow them to disintegrate, and willingly
leave the ashes by the wayside of awakening?

Like acquiescent fruit on an old peach tree
deliberately receiving, discreetly ripening,
so the refining movements of transformation
sweeten my heart into an orchard of peace.

~ Joyce Rupp

# *Coming Home*

*True self is the self with which we arrive on earth, the self that simply wants us to be who we were born to be.*

~ Parker Palmer

Of the valued books about how to approach old age, Kathleen Dowling Singh's *The Grace in Aging* tops my list. Singh dives deeply and doesn't "make nice." At the same time, she introduces hopeful messages with trusted, guiding truths that reorient us toward tranquility. These teachings reach into the heart of what later life involves if we are to be inwardly transformed. Singh urges her readers to be intentional about staying with this requirement. Doing so will enable us to grow freer and more at home with our truest self.

What does this transformation involve? And why is it "spiritual?" When we transform something we change it in a significant way so that it is not the same as before. Spiritual transformation changes something about our self, aiding its authenticity. Pamela D. Blair refers to our spiritual self as "an essential aspect of ourselves—you may call it the higher self, the real self, the center, or the God within. It feels like home when we connect with it." This spiritual dimension encompasses our inner world of thoughts, emotions, intuitions, dreams, along with life's external experiences of any and all kinds. The aging process invites us, implores us really, to be in touch with these areas, to live from the inside out.

As Blair noted, when we find our true self it feels like "home." We are always finding our way to this clear essence of who we are, but never more so than in our final years. In the film *The Wizard of Oz* when Dorothy is trying to find her way home, she asks Glinda the Good for a way to get there. Glinda replies: "Well, Dorothy, you were wise and good enough to help your friends to come here and find what was inside them all the time. That's true for you, also." Dorothy expresses confusion and asks, "Home? Inside of me? I don't understand." Then comes the response that those of us in our elder years hopefully hear. Glinda explains:

> Home is a place we all must find, child. It's not just a place where you eat or sleep. Home is knowing. Knowing your mind, knowing your heart, knowing your courage. If we know ourselves, we're always home, anywhere.

Spiritual transformation is about this *knowing*. When we are at home with ourselves, peace reigns. This peace, of course, comes at a price as often happens through an increased awareness of our illusions and depletions. As Singh points out:

> There are many who enter the end of life at ripe old ages, untapped and unexamined and filled with vir-

> tually as much confusion and unease as they were throughout all the decades of their lives. . . .
>
> To live a life of an elder is to ripen into being that is more than simply elderly, more than just old. It involves ripening into clear-eyed acceptance of the way things actually exist. This ripening involves, for each of us, many difficult reckonings in the multifaceted, multidimensional understanding that everything that can be lost will be lost.

As we age, we don't need to go looking for something to relinquish. About the time we think we've conquered our resistance to our forfeitures, another one shows up. Our teacher of transformation could be our physical self, or it might be our ego's voice insisting we are important, or that we be as lively and engaged as we were in the past. Spiritual transformation involves being willing to know how our ego operates so we can uncover the untruths we have about ourselves. Clarity about the true self alters us. We become increasingly authentic and serene, less demanding, more compassionate and humble. If we are open to this interior growth, a kind of metamorphosis takes place. This process of transformation is like a snake shedding its skin to allow for fuller development, a cocoon giving away its safe shelter to free a butterfly, or a maternal womb opening and bearing the pain required to push out fresh life.

An example of how this slow but beneficial growth takes place happened for me a week ago. Just a few lines from Eknath Easwaran reawakened my intention to rid myself of another illusion: "as long as you look at life through the spectacles of pain and pleasure, success and failure, praise and censure, you will never see life whole. One of the fatal flaws of the intellect is that it can thrive only in the land of duality." There it was—my intellect's insistence that I accept only what *I* want, only what *I* see as enjoyable, which is based on what comes across as pleasurable or not pleasurable in my either-or limited view. This awareness led me to a renewed desire to shed my judgment of what happens as being either for or against me.

With so little time left to live, I want to be as true as I can be, to stay open to growth while not chiding myself or succumbing to fault-finding for being less than perfect. In my late seventies, I noted this in my journal:

> Watch for the leaks in the roof. The storms in the heart easily bring rusted drips of hostility. There's not enough energy to get up there on the roof and patch the insistent cracks, but I can catch the drops before they reach and ruin what rests inside my room of love.

This room of love resides in our interior home, our true self. We deliberately claim our genuineness when we heed Louise Erdrich's counsel in "Advice to Myself."

> Pursue the authentic—decide first
> what is authentic,
> then go after it with all your heart.

# *Polishing the Mirror*

*Removing the dust of impurities and attachments*
*from the mirror of our heart-mind allows*
*the light of the spirit to be reflected.*
*As the layers become more transparent,*
*the light shines through us.*

~Rameshwar Das

Making our way to our genuine self entails both time and deliberate effort. Gradually we release what clutters and mars the interior self which is like a mirror reflecting our core goodness. "Polishing the mirror" describes clearing off what impedes us from activating our virtues. Kabir Helminski refers to this in *Living Presence*: "This mirror is like a sensitive screen on which appear our thoughts, desires, fears, expectations, and conditioning, and on which Spirit may also purely reflect." Helminski explains:

> By keeping the mirror of awareness clear we can begin to free ourselves of our compulsions and inappropriate thoughts and behaviors . . . our attachment to our opinions, our slavery to our likes and dislikes, our perpetual fear of loss. All of these

characteristics . . . to be transformed by the resonance of Love and the power of our essential Self.

For decades we swathed and protected our truer self with the person we thought we were. Now this self is uncovered, stripped like husks on an ear of corn, pulled back to reveal the golden kernels. By polishing our inner mirror we become increasingly aware of the sources of love within us—the attributes that reflect benevolence, integrity, patience, compassion, understanding, and numerous other positive qualities. As our transformation develops, these grace-filled assets are reflected more consistently in our attitudes and actions, which leads to a basic inner harmony, no matter what happens to us.

Polishing the mirror comes with a price tag. Some things have to be let go. This cost is referred to by Christian theologians as "kenosis," a Greek word for emptying out. This pricey depletion is exemplified in Jesus who poured his love out for humankind. The gift culminates by his selfless yielding to the painful crucifixion where he allows himself to be emptied of his human power and accepts the consequences of suffering. While our "deaths" or kenotic episodes are not that extensive and excruciating, we may well feel dreadful pain when being stripped of a former ability to manage how we wanted to live and who we planned to be (Philippians 2:1–2).

The kenotic pain of late life most often involves a change or an adjustment in our mental, emotional, and spiritual capabilities. Whether we choose or rebel against being polished, the unwanted issues of aging will thrust us into situations with the potential for this to happen. Throughout the centuries, philosophers, writers, and teachers have used challenging metaphors to describe this movement of spiritual growth in which the mirror of self becomes cleared of its crusty blemishes.

St. John of the Cross uses *purification by fire* to describe how the mirror becomes cleared: "The soul that is in a state of transformation of love may be said to be . . . like the log of wood that is continually assailed by the fire; and the acts of this soul are the flame that arises from the fire of love."

Carol Orsborn uses *sandpaper* in writing about transformation: "the abrasion of life has effected the removal of all but the essential. Every fact on the list—the chaos, the rejection, the wounding: grains of sand that scrape and file to reveal the smoothed contours of what had been hidden, waiting to be revealed." Frank Cunningham refers to "sifting out the chaff, watching for that quick glint of flame" as we seek to encourage growth beyond strongly held opinions and conclusions. Job uses nakedness to speak about the inner clearance that occurs: "Naked I came from my mother's womb, and naked shall I return there" (Job 1:22).

The early Sumerian myth of Inanna refers to her inner polishing by describing how this queen has to strip off her crown, jewels, robe, and inner garments until she is completely naked before entering the Underworld's transformative darkness. Jesus uses parables to emphasize this aspect of spiritual growth: a seed sloughing off its protective shell, a tree being pruned to encourage new growth, selling *everything* to go in search of a treasure buried in a field. A tough image comes from the Persian poet Rumi's *pickaxe,* the tool he suggests for casting aside illusory debris to find the wealth of truest love beneath it.

These radical images indicate the kind of inner alteration expected in later life. The loss, depletion, and increasing vulnerability of old age will grow us spiritually in greater or lesser degree, depending on our receptivity to emptying, purifying, and polishing. Beatrice Bruteau described this required process in *The Easter Mysteries*:

> Transformation is something we all crave. This is what we are looking for under the guises of the many things we do. . . . We really want to lose ourselves, and yet we cling to ourselves. . . . But to realize ourselves as indefinable, of course, we would have to stop identifying ourselves by all these descriptions to which we are attached. . . . Many people will describe themselves in terms of the position or success they have achieved. . . . Now, can we transcend these descriptions? Can we strip ourselves naked of adjectives? If we do, what will we have left? Nothing, it seems. And that *nothing* is just the point.

Freeing one's self of descriptions came through Gregory's interview at age eighty-three. A highly qualified professional with a humble ego, he continues to assist people on society's margins. To the question of how he wanted to be remembered after death, Gregory responded, "I have no need to be remembered."

When we encourage the "I" to sit down and be quiet, the obstructive residue of our inner self dissolves. The Eternal Light then shines more brightly through our being. Need we ask for anything more?

# *Seeing in the Dark*

*In a dark time, the eye begins to see.*

~ Theodore Roethke

When Elderhood arrives, we pass beyond the dawn and noon to the evening of our life. We enter the twilight stage known as "dusk" in the world of nature when daylight dwindles and slides slowly into an ebony silence. At dusk, a peaceful mood prevails before nighttime arrives. Most everything seems to slow down. The spirit of elders reflects this serene atmosphere, but many of us will plunge—at least momentarily—into the dark of night. With the insistent, constant adjustments of aging, we are bound to have times of feeling somewhat disoriented or lost. These uninvited feelings come with nighttime territory.

Darkness is not always negative, any more than light is always positive. Think of the fertile darkness of the womb swathing a fetus and of blistering sunlight shriveling a robust garden. Rather than total obscurity, Elderhood's darkness usually involves more of a grainy landscape, a film-like fogginess that hangs over mind and heart. A psychological term for this is *liminality*—being between two places, a stage of "in-between." This gloomy, liminal space conjures a mood rife with doldrums where we wrangle with loss and resist debilities. We are no longer who we were and not yet who we will be. Questions surface about what meaning can be found in the midst of accumulating impediments. Enthusiasm wanes. Ennui visits us. The loss of a secured tethering weakens emotional and spiritual strongholds. Life allows for little that satisfies. In this darkness, a sense of the value of one's present life disappears. It's like stumbling through a forest at midnight.

Being in a state of liminality might involve a long stretch or brief in-and-out occurrences. I recently journaled about one of these short interludes:

> Yesterday felt like "lost soul day." I couldn't find myself anywhere. I was a lone cloud floating through a gauzy sky, wandering about in fruitless activity; a stray dog searching for a buried bone. But nothing I sought satisfied me. I never did know what led me into that brief exile, but it felt a lot like the long stretches of darkness that people describe.

Unlike my miniscule experience of liminality, Lara's went on and on. When I met this late-in-life woman at a retreat, she told of a lingering, excruciating darkness that swooped in and snatched both faith and joy:

> I face chronic declining lung health. I've been so discouraged this past month with little energy, difficult ongoing coughing, and can't find a way to stop the loss of interest in life. . . . I long to feel a sense of hope. . . . Wondering where God is and about how to believe He is here in my loss. I just don't feel His presence.

When Helen Luke relates the story of Odysseus in *Old Age*, she makes special note of the blind seer Tiresias whose physical sightlessness enables his inner vision to discern the wisdom he will share with Odysseus. It is the far-seeing Tiresias who advises the sea-faring Odysseus of the difficult journey he has to make in order to reclaim the virtues he lost as a result of his boastful arrogance and cruel attacks on his enemies.

To be old is to accept life's unwanted darkness as having the potential for spiritual growth. We learn to trust that each physical, spiritual, relational, and psychological encounter brings with it possibilities for growth. As our inner eye becomes accustomed to this darkness, insights slowly begin to appear, much like the way in which our physical eyes gradually adjust to a darkened room and slowly discern the objects in it.

In our shadowy, inner room, we detect certain behaviors of ours, such as clutching people or things too tightly. We gain awareness of having more inner strength than we realized, and we concede that we'll never be able to stop bad things happening to good people. We come to believe our compassionate presence is valued more than we thought it was and become aware that the Holy One's presence does not always involve consoling feelings. We learn we are still able to be kind, regardless of our physical situation, that we are capable of healing our wounds, and that darkness need not demolish our hope or lessen our compassion.

In a Nazi death camp, Jewish psychologist Viktor Frankl felt beaten down physically and psychically. He struggled to find a spark of hope and was at the point of surrendering to death. In *Man's Search for Meaning* he describes that moment:

> In a last violent protest against the hopelessness of imminent death, I sensed my spirit piercing through the enveloping gloom. I felt it transcend that hopeless, meaningless world, and from somewhere I heard a victorious "Yes" in answer to my question of the existence of an ultimate purpose. At that moment a light was lit in a distant farmhouse, which stood on the horizon as if painted there, in the midst of the miserable grey of a dawning morning in Bavaria. "*Et lux in tenebris lucet*"—and the light shineth in the darkness.

In that graced moment Frankl regained his desire to live. When our liminality remains bleak it may be that we, too, have only a faint light in the distance to keep our hope alive.

The fermentation of wine takes place in the dark. Too much exposure to light spoils the process of transforming crushed grapes into wine. For us in our final years, the unwanted aspects of aging provide the crushed grapes for our spiritual transformation. As with grapes, we are removed from our secure base and tossed into a fermenting darkness. There our transformation occurs—an ongoing process through which we become like delicious wine, clear and robust, heart-felt nourishment for those who imbibe our loving presence and inborn goodness.

# *The Natural Monastery*

*It is a pity we have lost the tidings of our souls,*
*we shall have to go in search of them again.*

~ Mary Ann Shaffer and Annie Barrows

Going in search of communication with our souls during our elder years sounds a bit dramatic, doesn't it? We do not lose our souls, but we can and do occasionally lose touch with their "tidings," their voice and resonance, their inherent wisdom. As we age, finding our way to what truly counts becomes vital. More than ten years ago, Beatrice Bruteau urged her readers to "find our way back." The way to do this, she insisted, is through contemplation, which involves "holding still" for a while. Well, holding still is certainly something we older people are capable of doing. We naturally move into a slower paced life, which prevents us from participating in the cultural "hurry."

Deceleration is part of our eldering years. Everything takes longer to do—getting ourselves dressed, moving from place to place, preparing and eating meals, making that phone call, writing that note. This unhurried pace assists us in being less distracted and more mindful so that we are less prone to misplace items or forget what we went into the next room to do. (Ever tried to get out of the car while still wearing a seatbelt?) Less activity, increased solitude, fewer pressures to push us toward productive accomplishments—these ease our dashing about. They allow us to be attentive to what is within and around us.

Ezra Bayda suggests that this phase of life gifts us with what he terms "the natural monastery." According to Bayda, we have the option of shifting our priorities as we come to terms with our remaining years. This author of *Aging for Beginners* recognizes how our focus changes direction from being constantly busy to devoting more of our attention "to a deeper quest—the essence of monastery life. We can prioritize having fewer distractions, leaving more time for meditation, prayer, reading, and writing, as well as being in nature."

When I took the Bullet Train from Narita airport to Tokyo, Japan, I arrived there in what seemed like a nanosecond. I was happy about the fast travel but disappointed that the high speed blurred the landscape. I barely caught a view of anything. Similarly, our inner vision catches the clarity and the subtle nuances of what we behold only when we slow our pace. If our life moves like a speeding train inside or outside of us, we're going to miss seeing what resides there. When we go slowly we are more apt to be with what we are presently doing, more mindful of the "now," which is where we learn, grow, and celebrate life's wonders. As William Martin puts it:

> We are slowing down,
> but waking up.
> We are producing less,
> but learning more.

We are doing less,
and experiencing more.

Widows, widowers, and other single elders would probably say they have plenty of silence and wish for more activity. The kind of silence I suggest is not the lack of sound that comes from living alone, but rather an inward quiet that allows us to reflect and be present to the deeper part of ourselves. Without this silence, we skim along on the surface of life, resisting what requires our attention, and we miss what gives meaning and clarity to daily living. It is this kind of positive, inner stillness that Robert Sordello addresses in *Silenc*e:

> Each time we venture into the realm of Silence consciously, not merely by accident, our soul is strengthened and a feeling-with-clarity emerges. When we become just a bit more alert within this realm, we discover something paradoxical. This realm of Silence is filled with currents of activity. We do not enter into loneliness or isolation but into the deeper feeling of communing. Our soul feels full, whole, and completely within its own milieu. . . . Each thing we perceive in Silence shines forth with new clarity and integrity.

What could happen during our chosen silence? Perhaps we focus on reviewing some part of our life to discover what we enjoyed, where we met defeat and re-found hope. We uncover reasons to rejoice in people who assisted us in becoming who we are. Patient listening enables us to come to terms with unresolved issues. Our silence can be a sacred, wordless communing with a presence larger than ourselves, one that feels comforting, like a parent holding a newborn. This intentional quiet time often leads us to gratitude.

Oceanographers have researched and shared their findings about the amazing life that exists within the immense waters on our planet. We humans have a vast expanse of life within us that also remains to be explored. We are the oceanographers of our inner being. In our elder years we have the time and opportunity to explore those depths, to trust we will find what increases our understanding and appreciation of the life we've been given.

Once we become accustomed to entering into silence, we can more easily slip into it each day for a period of stillness, to receive the peace that strengthens our being. Silence and solitude need never be our enemies, surely not in our elder years. Kathleen Dowling Singh assures us that "just as we enter love by being love, we enter silence by being silence. A warm, embracing, very present silence. A refuge. The ultimate old-age home."

When we participate in the natural monastery, a certain refreshing spaciousness develops. It may take a while, but gradually interior stillness becomes the norm. We slide into it effortlessly. The more we live in this contemplative mode the more we find "the tidings of our soul."

As we enjoy the slower pace and pause for breathing, we recover inner strength. When we develop the habit of being still and listening to our hidden self, we meet the Friend who waits to accompany us through whatever happens next.

# XII

# Serenity

## "Perspective"

Old age assists me
to put into perspective
what I've striven for
and sought to possess.
As I cast a glance backward
to what has been,
confining cravings weaken
in their claim.

The later years free me
from a tight grasping.
I discard the firm grip on status
and success,
the false hope to be revered
by differing voices
and the futile desire
to erase life's uncertainty.

When clutching and grasping
end their reign,
what was overlooked rises gently
to the surface.
My aged physical eyes perceive
less distinctly
but the view from the aging heart
sharpens.

I recognize and welcome a
shrouded Presence
mingling with the gossamer
of my immortal soul.
While external identity gradually
fades from view,
I let it slip away, trusting that
only love will last.

~ Joyce Rupp

# *When the Time Comes*

*I am moving*
*Toward a new freedom*
*Born of detachment*
*And a sweeter grace—*
*Learning to let go.*

~ May Sarton

After Queen Elsa sang "Let it go, let it go, let it go" in the film *Frozen*, people of all ages were belting it out with gusto. Perhaps they did so because most everyone carries something that hinders or burdens their spirit. Letting go profits us at any age but emerges as an essential response in Elderhood. We've lived a long time and collected a lot, not just materially, but immaterially, too—ideas and opinions, likes and dislikes. We know what we prefer and are quite sure of what we do not prefer.

In mid-life I encountered the spiritual principle of detachment while doing graduate studies at a Buddhist University. Among the many things I learned, one of the most important was how humans often create their unhappiness by either clinging to what they want or resisting what they do not want—emotional responses of "grasping and aversion." When we respond by clutching our preferences or by trying to get rid of unavoidable obstacles, we remain unfree, lacking inner harmony. Thirty years later, I value this wisdom more than ever. Being released from my ways and wishes is no longer an option. It is a requirement.

If we spend any time at all with resources from religious traditions related to spiritual growth, we will soon be urged to consider practicing detachment and to accept the necessity of "letting go." Detachment frees us from our desire that the present and future give us what we insist upon having. Is there ever a day without some reminder that we elders have to let go of this or that? Consider the endless stream of what can be clung to: physical appearances and trying to look younger, the hope of outsmarting or outlasting others, thinking of self as worthless and unappreciated or as superior, material items, moldy angers and ancient gripes, a yearning to be "on stage" instead of gladly being in the audience, hurtful speech, meddling or interfering, coveting what others have or are, refusal to revise philosophies or religious beliefs that harm rather than help, and anything else we either tightly grasp or stubbornly avoid.

Seng-Ts'an, the seventh-century Eastern philosopher taught that "the Great Way isn't difficult for those who are unattached to their preferences. Let go of longing and aversion, and everything will be perfectly clear." Angeles Arrien approaches this another way: *Be open to outcome, not attached to outcome.* She then clarifies that "to detach" does not suggest giving up, or to no longer caring about others, nor does it lessen enjoying what we do. Detaching means acknowledging likes and dislikes without allowing them to control or squash our inner peace. We openly receive what we value—not forcing the results or insisting everything has to work to our advantage. We let go when the time arrives for us to do so.

Detachment is the quality that helps us forego our demands that life should give us all we expect, that we're entitled to it and deserve to have it. No matter how hard we've worked, no matter how diligently we've cared for our health, no matter how much we've tried to be the best person we could be, we will not be able to control how old age alters us. The truth is, no matter how much effort we make, things are not always going to go our way. We cannot keep people from dying when it is their time to depart. In spite of our attempts to have a youthful body and perfect memory, these things will change. Even if we struggle endlessly to be fully independent, we're eventually going to require some assistance. If we refuse to accept these unwanted results, we add to our discontent.

When we are attached to what cannot be—insisting we have to have it—we lessen our emotional balance. Insignificant trifles can dampen our peacefulness, such as being upset when a friend neglects to call, voicing constant dismay over the kind of food served in a residential dining room, fretting over someone's negative comment about what we're wearing, or grumbling about how long we sit and wait at a medical appointment.

Much larger things, of course, send our emotions into a tailspin if we are attached to the outcome, such as when medication keeping arthritic pain at bay is no longer effective; a best friend with terminal cancer slips away; our years of faithful communication with relatives are ignored when the family fails to include us in a significant celebration, or the grandson we dearly love remains addicted to drugs.

Painful emotions naturally arise. We ought not to deny their presence because they will continue to fester if unattended. At the same time, if we choose to give them some distance (detach) we are not swallowed by them. This happened to Marilyn in her late seventies when a teenager stole her car. Not only was her car stolen and vandalized, but she also lost valued material items she kept in it. One day when Marilyn was again bemoaning what had happened, her son spoke two sentences that served to loosen her attachment: *It is already gone, Mom. Let it go.* Marilyn told me, "Those words are now the mantra that I choose to live by for the rest of my life."

We can't always avoid having a disabling disease, we can't always choose where we live, or decide what our days will bring, but we *can* change the way we respond to what seems like an intrusion or invasion of our life. If we heed the following suggestion of Mary Oliver's "In Blackwater Woods," inner peace has a much better chance of dwelling in us. Oliver described three essential things we must do:

> To live in this world
> you must be able
> to do three things:
> to love what is mortal;
> to hold it
> against your bones knowing
> your own life depends on it;
> and, when the time comes to let it go,
> to let it go.

# *The Radical Response*

*Do not brace yourself against suffering.*
*Try to close your eyes and surrender yourself,*
*as if to a great loving energy.*

~ Teilhard De Chardin

Yesterday when I walked through the woods, I spied a bird's nest resting by the side of the path. Perhaps the nest had been torn from its nook by recent strong winds. Whatever had lifted and brought it down, the former home lay there abandoned, a circle of unrequited love. The bird's labor of gathering dried grasses, cottonwood down, papery leaves, and tiny twigs to form a container for birthing and sheltering no longer mattered. The nest had become a dashed dream. We humans also have those aspects of life that we worked diligently to develop and keep strong but they no longer serve the purpose we intended. We could try to restore them back to their original purpose, but like a bird unable to return her fallen nest to the branch, we cannot restore what is no longer possible. We then have two choices—we can rail against what fled or has been taken from us, or we can surrender to the reality of no longer having what we hoped to retain until our death.

When Helen Luke writes about old age in relation to Shakespeare's *King Lear*, she reflects on the king's imprisonment and notes that "He is growing old." Luke then elaborates:

> As a man grows old, his body weakens, his powers fail, his sight perhaps is dimmed, his hearing fades, or his power to move is taken from him, In one way or another he is *imprisoned*, and the moment of choice will come to him. Will he fight this confining process or will he go to meet it in the spirit of King Lear—embrace it with love, with eagerness even?

*With eagerness.* That seems daunting. We might not be enthusiastic about the unwanted consequences of Elderhood, but we are wise to follow Helen Luke's suggestion that we submit to the vicissitudes of our old age. Submitting or surrendering sounds severe when we first discover that being spiritually transformed requires this radical interior response. Each significant loss expands the quarry where the gold of our true essence is found and refined through aging if we give ourselves to it. To lose the health we've known, to experience increasing vulnerability, to watch as the circle of loved ones closes in, we're bound to feel the bitter taste of sorrow, maybe a period of depression, not wanting to accept any of it. What might we do to avoid being devastated by certain depletions? We can practice our ability to surrender with each reckoning that bends our will and our heart.

A few years before his death at age eighty, respected German theologian Karl Rahner, SJ, agreed to an interview, which was published under the title *I Remember.* Here's how he responded when asked about his views on death.

> They say of St. Albert the Great that at the end of his life he forgot all his magnificent theology. . . . He could only pray the "Hail Mary." Good, if this happens to you, then you must cope with it too. Once you are on your death bed, then everything does indeed cease—perhaps even your ability to react to such a situation. If even this is taken from you, all the better. Then, I believe, you find yourself all the more in God's hands, and no longer in your own. And you are better protected and more secure in God's hands than when you think you must be in control at all costs.

As we discover and claim the ground of our being where true Love resides, we find the courage to make the radical choice of surrender. This is what we do when we feel we have nowhere to go but to place ourselves in the trusting care of a Presence greater than ourselves to sustain us in our misery, loneliness, humiliations, and excruciating vulnerabilities—a Presence to assure us of ultimately not being alone, for strength and an ability to be at peace. Whether we give ourselves over to Jesus, to the Higher Power of *Alcoholics Anonymous,* to the saints, or to the mysterious Love guiding the cosmos, in surrendering ourselves we trust we'll receive protection, safety, refuge, and comfort.

I first experienced this at age forty. I lay on my back on a gurney, heading into surgery to have an ovarian cyst removed. Soon I would know if the cyst was malignant. As I lay there waiting, I had a vivid recollection of Jesus hanging on the cross, surrendering himself in his final hour to his trusted Holy One. That memory moved me to pray: "Into your hands I surrender myself." As I repeated this, such a marvelous calm came over me. I felt held by a strengthening Love, assured that no matter what the outcome, all would be well. And it was.

As the years sail by, I've come to a solid trust that within myself and in every parcel of life a mysterious and loving Presence exists in different degrees of intensity. This ever present, all-caring, and all-carrying Love supports and energizes the essence of humans and non-humans. Handing ourselves over rarely comes quickly, but when we finally do this, what a difference it makes. More than twenty years ago, I met frail Sister Connie Bader coming down the corridor with her walker, oxygen pack in a front basket, tubes in her nostrils. She told me how despondent she had been several months earlier when she realized her good health would never return. She felt miserable and depressed for weeks. Sleep evaded her until one night she cried out, "God, I can't do this anymore. I'm turning it all over to you. I can't worry, be angry, or fight anymore."

No sooner had Sister Connie done this when a pervasive peace engulfed her, one that never left after her surrender. In the moment of "turning it all over," she experienced what Quaker Thomas Kelley taught: "Self is emptied into God and God in-fills it."

Surrendering in old age becomes increasingly frequent until the moment arrives when there's nothing left to release except the last exhalation. We will be ready for this final yielding because we will have become a pro at surrendering.

# *An Unshakeable Balance*

*Grant me the serenity*
*to accept the things I cannot change,*
*courage to change the things I can,*
*and wisdom to know the difference.*

~ Reinhold Niebuhr

In preparing to write this reflection on the serenity accessible to us in old age, I returned for the umpteenth time to a chapter on "Equanimity" in Christina Feldman's *Boundless Heart*. She describes with both eloquence and realism how to acquire "inner stillness and poise in the midst of chaos." Feldman refers to equanimity as "understanding what it means to stand in the midst of all experience with unshakeable balance, to be responsive yet unbroken." This author recognizes that life includes change and unpredictability, yet she assures us of our inner resilience, the ability to not be overcome by aging's capricious happenings.

Feldman's invitation "to learn to abide in calm in the midst of agitation, to abide in peace in the midst of conflict, to abide in balance in the midst of chaos" echoes the equanimity that grounds each of the lines of Reinhold Niebuhr's prayer. According to Feldman, equanimity is:

> a responsive way of meeting our shifting life, our changing body and mind, and all of the events we are asked to embrace. It is not developed in the most sublime and peaceful moments in our lives but in the moments we feel most agitated and shattered, most lost and unbalanced. It is a practice of meeting and understanding the uncertainty and unpredictability we so fear and a commitment to the freedom of our own hearts in the midst of it all.

The serenity that accompanies equanimity rests on accepting disturbances we cannot eliminate when they intrude on our lives. We first make efforts to alleviate the disruptions and suffering. When this proves to be out of our control, we then let it be. I learned the value of this from a retreatant's comment about her husband's leukemia when the prognosis was terminal: "*Let be* helps me more than *let go*."

In the epic *Lord of the Rings*, Gandalf the wizard urges a similar wisdom. The hobbit Frodo laments, "I wish it need not have happened in my time." Gandalf responds, "So do I and so do all who live to see such times. But that is not for them to decide. All we have to decide is what to do with the time that is given to us."

While visiting my community's motherhouse, I noticed how Sister Karen uses some of the time given to her. For more than a year now, she pauses daily by a large window, intent on looking out at the roof. She becomes immersed in the sight of one mute, lifeless yellow warbler lying in the rusty eave. She observes the small bird's body shrink in size and fade in color as it rests on the inaccessible space. Pondering with amazement the measured dissolvement of the warbler's body, the eighty-three-year-old accepts that her body, too, will follow that same dissolving pattern. This gazing enables her to find a balance between the life she dearly loves and the future death awaiting her.

It takes courage to stand at the window of our senescence and accept that death will reach us before too many years. At almost one hundred, when asked about his coming death, the poet Stanley Kunitz replied, "I think all the forces, all the energies of my life are converging and that I won't know what my destiny is until a compelling voice takes over and it says, *This is the right path for you to go. Follow me.* And I'll go."

I sensed a similar "unshakeable balance" with Thomas who was in hospice at home. When I asked how he was feeling he whispered in a strained voice, "I'm not angry." Even so, the tall, gaunt man shed tears when asked what it was like for him to lose so much. He had been an avid golfer, generous community volunteer, loving husband, and delighted grandfather. Thomas could have sunk into anger at the prospect of dying from lung disease at age seventy-five but he chose to submit to the inevitable after medical measures no longer worked. In his acceptance, Thomas found an "unshakeable balance," the peace of equanimity.

Whatever our current experience of aging, we will have moments when we face choosing how to meet the time left to us—when to stand up and face the foe or succumb to what must be, when to keep up the hunt for alleviation or swallow hard and move on to the unalterable. Making decisions such as these, of course, affects our relationships. Living into old age with an unshakeable balance gifts not only ourselves but also those around us. Kathleen Dowling Singh advises, "If we are to claim the last years of life as years that hold the possibility of awakening into equanimity and lightness, into the very embodiment of grace, we need to bear witness to the ripening of that possibility. Not only would it be a blessing for each of us, it would be a blessing for a world starved for such witnessing."

I'm reminded of this when I walk near a tall tree in Red Feather Prairie. The slim tree is completely white, nary a trace of bark. The half dozen branches have long ago lost their twigs. This tree stands by itself in a section of tall grasses. What I've noticed is that the tree has not lost a purpose—its availability for birds to sit near the top where they have an overview of the land. The tree provides a welcoming place of rest. This is what we elders can be, even in our last phase of life—a resting place of equanimity for people whose days sag with stressful work or other burdens. We offer our wordless, peaceable presence. We serve as a reminder of inner serenity.

A quote of Thomas Merton's has often instilled in me a desire to have that kind of serenity, to trust that by "doing nothing" I am contributing to the growth of self and the welfare of others. James Finley quotes Merton as saying, "How does an apple ripen? It just sits in the sun." Finley then reminds the reader that an apple cannot ripen "by tightening its jaw in order to find itself the next morning miraculously large, red, ripe and juicy." The apple *accepts* being on the tree, waits for the sun and rain to provide for its preparation in being a source of nurturance. What an inviting image of equanimity, the peace of acceptance.

We need every pulse of equanimity when old age bangs on the door. If we choose to live with what we cannot change, whether this involves a person, a health issue, or a world situation, we come to know the unshakeable balance that derives from "let be."

# *Love Is What Counts*

*At the end of the road they will ask me*
*Have you lived? Have you loved?*
*And not saying a word I will open my heart*
*full of names.*

~ Dom Pedro Casaldàliga

The quote above belongs to a Portuguese bishop who spent his priestly life dedicated to respecting and loving impoverished people. If anyone believed love is what counts and put this into practice, it was Pedro Casaldàliga. When he died, his body lay in a plain wooden casket with an opened Bible placed on his bare feet. Seeing this powerful image on the internet quickened a desire in my aged heart to express that kind of staunch love.

At eighty-one years old, my energy and physical abilities become more limited, but the love in my heart remains limitless. I can live and love generously right where I am and be intentional about extending love in diverse ways. You can do this, too. We elders have plenty of time to waste on loving. This gift costs nothing except forgetting about ourselves for a while and becoming a channel with no stipulations as to how our love goes forth and is received.

When our love expands, we aid not just others but also ourselves. As Teilhard de Chardin proposed, "It is through love and within love that we must look for the deepening of our deepest self, in the life-giving coming together of humankind. Love is the free and imaginative outpouring of the spirit over all unexplored paths." When we feel despondent about the condition of our society and doubt whether world peace and human well-being will ever occur globally, we can move beyond this hopelessness and trust that each touch of love extended outward strengthens the virtues existing in humanity.

Awareness is a vital key. Being alert and believing in the worth of our self-giving motivates us to contribute to world-transformation by manifesting our ripened virtues such as generosity, kindness, patience, forgiveness, understanding, acceptance, and friendliness. When our love expands, these virtues flow from us as naturally as untainted water from a mountain spring.

Eighty-eight-year-old Andrew has taken this truth into himself and acts on it. He tells me that he wakes up many nights, for an hour or more. Instead of being distressed by this, he uses it for good, for love. "The night is important to me," Andrew explains. "This is my time to send love out to my friends, to the world. I open myself to truth, to a cosmic love, a Source bigger than myself, for the transformation of the world."

This movement of interrelationship progresses with the increased transparency of our truest self, a mirror of divine love. We grow in being free to share our love as best we can. In *New Seeds of Contemplation*, Thomas Merton describes this as moving toward a relationship with the Holy One where our self and the Divine are no longer distinct beings: "What happens is that the separate entity that is *you* apparently disappears and nothing seems to be left but a pure freedom indistinguishable from infinite Freedom, love identified with Love. Not two loves, one waiting for the other, striving for the other, seeking for the other, but Love, Loving in Freedom."

There's no need to compare who loves better or which way of self-giving surpasses another's. Simply allowing love to travel from our ripened goodness into the lives of those around us is what matters and makes a difference. We demonstrate this light-filled quality in our own unique manner as our goodness flows forth through our personalities and spiritualities. Some of us share our love by being kind, thoughtful, and interested in how life affects others. Some of us express our care by being affirming, charitable, or showing empathy in being present prayerfully with those who suffer.

When I read the following by Bede Griffiths in *Return to the Centre,* the Benedictine monk gave me words to express what I believe to be the definitive goal of Elderhood:

> The ultimate Mystery of being, the ultimate Truth, is Love. . . . Love giving itself, losing itself and finding itself in love, and Love returning to itself, giving itself back in love—this is the eternal pattern of the universe. Every creature in the depth of its being is a desire, a longing for Love, and is drawn by Love to give itself in love. This is its coming into being, this response to the drawing of Love. At the same time it is being continually drawn to give itself in love, to surrender to the attraction of Love, and so the rhythm of the universe is created. . . . There is

> a continual dance of love, a continual going and returning.

Growing and maturing in this pattern of receiving love/giving love, we live in such a way that our belief about this is readily apparent. We become increasingly persons of great love until all that we are and do flows from this rhythm. We shed our need for self-importance and embrace the joy of being a person in whom the eternal Love and our love mingle so completely that the boundaries between the two dissolve. Think of the ebb and flow of an ocean. If we sit on the seashore long enough, quietly enough, we become completely absorbed, losing our sense of self, entrained with the rhythm of the sound of the waves moving back and forth, in and out. When I experience this and then reluctantly leave that precious intertwining to tend to other parts of my life, the ocean's rhythm continues inside of me. I close my eyes, open my heart, and there I am again with the oneness I felt.

We may never reach the point where we "love perfectly" but our concern about self can steadily diminish. Our eyes gradually see only the goodness in another person. Our hands reach to give without concern about what we might lose. Our heart opens wide to be a portal of hospitality.

At death we slip through the thin veil on the wings of freedom, merging with the One Great Love who urged us throughout our existence, "Remember to come home."

# EPILOGUE

## Making the Last Crossing

*"Migration," he whispers. He once heard migration defined as "a bridge"—a bridge that birds, animals and nomads crossed as the world behind them became uninhabitable. A bridge that vanished behind them as they went, leaving them no choice but the far side. So cross, says a voice. Which he now hears as his own.*

~ David Duncan

All of life consists of transitions that transport us to the next stage of our existence. But the final decades are especially relevant because this era is our last opportunity to come into the fullness of our self. Every transition takes us somewhere on our lifelong path. We do not stand still in this life unless we become a lump of clay and refuse to budge. Some respond this way by denial or a strong resistance to the changes of old age, but most elders bravely give themselves to the process of moving farther along this path.

Think of the countless transitions, large and small, that you've known in your lifetime. Why is it that as we get older, these moves toward something new tend to become more challenging? It would seem that, having had the experience of numerous transitions, they'd become almost "ho hum" for us. Not so. Moving to a smaller living space, getting a new phone, having a longtime physician retire and finding a new one—these changes can wear out and worry a person just thinking about having to deal with them. It's no wonder that we might be concerned as to how we will experience the last months or years of our life.

Four metaphors of transition keep me bouncing back to hope when I have a dismal day or if disquiet creeps in when I think about how and when I'll reach the end of my physical journey. These images resurrect my courage and provide an assurance that our ripening years and physical ending are a natural part of existence.

### *"Migration"*

The first metaphor is that of seasonal migration. When I entered my seventies I became fascinated with this annual feat, how waterfowl, insects, fish, mammals, and other creatures choose to move from one secure, comfortable place to another, a move that often requires intense stamina. I wonder if this fascination has something to do with the inner migration taking place within myself as the season of old age urges me to make one last migratory passage, one that requires inner resilience and courage. A migratory flight from which I will not return.

Ellen Levine's book *Up Close: Rachel Carson* includes a letter written by Carson to her friend Dorothy less than a year before Carson died of cancer in 1964:

> But most of all I shall remember the Monarchs, that unhurried westward drift of one small winged form

after another, each drawn by some invisible force. We talked a little about their migration, their life history. Did they return? We thought not; for most, at least, this was the closing journey of their lives.

But it occurred to me this afternoon, remembering, that it had been a happy spectacle, that we had felt no sadness when we spoke of the fact that there would be no return. And rightly—for when any living thing has come to the end of its life cycle we accept that end as natural.

For the Monarch, that cycle is measured in a known span of months. For ourselves, the measure is something else, the span of which we cannot know. But the thought is the same: when that intangible cycle has run its course it is a natural and not unhappy thing that a life comes to its end.

This is what those brightly fluttering bits of life taught me this morning. I found a deep happiness in it—so, I hope, may you.

*"The Bridge"*

The second metaphor is that of a bridge. We elders have moved through numerous transitions both inner and outer by the time we step into Elderhood. Some of our past bridges helped us to move along as we dragged ourselves over and beyond them. Other transitions attracted us. We sprinted forward over those bridges with eager anticipation. Sometimes we became stuck for a while. Each of these crossings, whether chosen or thrust upon us, proceeded to alter our life in some substantial way. Step by step, year by year, change after change, we made our way along and through the passageways. Now we are on the final stretch. For some of us that bridge may be lengthy and take us to a hundred years. For others, the distance grows quite short. Wherever we are on the bridge of life, each of us will eventually arrive at the point where the passageway culminates.

As we moved through life, our significant bridge-crossings progressed in the pattern described by Kathleen Fischer: "All transitions follow a similar cycle. The process takes us from ending and relinquishment, through emptiness and darkness, to fresh life and new beginnings." The view at the end of the bridge with its new beginnings remains hidden. We cannot see very far ahead, unable to detect how much farther we've yet to go in making it to the end, or what it will be like to do this. We can only conjecture and count on what lies beyond, trusting it will be a second birthing, a new life of refreshing freedom after we breathe our last.

### *"The Old Interior Angel"*

We have within us the courage to make our final crossing. We have our "old interior angel," the one David Whyte described when he initially sat paralyzed by fear, unable to walk across a wobbly, wooden bridge without railings that hung high above a Himalayan chasm. Whyte finally overcame his terror of the unstable bridge after an

> old mountain woman
> with her stooped gait...
> Small feet shuffling...
> went straight across

that shivering chaos
of wood
and broken steel
in one movement.

It was then Whyte knew he had the courage to do the same.

The old woman's trust in her ability to do what put fear and dread in the poet Whyte becomes a symbol for us. As we face the final years of what appears daunting, we gain the impetus to go forward when we remember and trust our inner strength and ability to do so. We have our own interior angel to accompany us across our final bridge, however wobbly the way might be, however deep and intimidating the chasm of the crossing appears.

### *"The Zen Garden"*

The fourth metaphor for the final stage of life comes from William Marvin's watercolor painting of a sculpture in a Zen garden. When I first saw the image in his book, *Grace Notes*, the scene spoke to me of what empowers us to make the last crossing peacefully. The simple sculpture consists of two objects. Pliable, braided willow branches are bent to form a half circle, creating a high arc like a rainbow, with each end of the branches attached to the ground. Underneath this arc sits a solid granite boulder, an image of strength and endurance. In our final years, we elders especially require the inner balance of these two—the bendable and the unbendable, the moveable and the immoveable, in order for peace to reign within ourselves. This sculpture sits in front of a dense forest that hides what resides within it, a reminder that we cannot know what awaits beyond our last transition.

Both of the sculpture's characteristics residing in us are essential to accompany us to the other side of this life. Suppleness and malleability enable us to remain open to change and to accept alterations in body, mind, and spirit. At the same time, we remain solidly grounded in the durability of a well-secured soul, a spirituality that keeps our peace unshakeable. "Spiritual hardiness"—that's how Marsha Sinetar terms this boulder-like quality to indicate "strength born of union with the divine Love, or the God of our understanding."

### *"Our Ripened, Solidly Gounded in Love Soul"*

When I walk through the woods, I often meet an older man. As I pass by him, his face lights up with a beautiful smile. He looks directly at me, touches his right hand to his heart, then holds this hand out toward me as he calls out a cheerful "Good morning." This gesture is how I hope to be as an elder until the time comes to move beyond those last steps on the rickety bridge of old age. I want to open my deepest self to all I meet—people, creation, every parcel of life—embodying a welcoming love residing within the One Great Love existing in everyone and everything.

As we make our final crossing, may the following wisdom of Steven Charleston's in *Spirit Wheel* be our daily affirmation.

> I will not waver in my trust
> that whatever may come
> In the end the Spirit of goodness and mercy
> Will be waiting for me on the other side.

# Study Guide

*A useful bibliography can be found in "Discussion Guides" on the Joyce Rupp website at www.joycerupp.com.*

## Introduction—"Now I Become Myself"

If you were developing a curriculum for a course on Elderhood, what five central topics would you be sure to include? Why would you choose these particular ones?

Consider May Sarton's poem. Which of the lines relate to your aging?

What are some surprising aspects of your current life?

If you were to draw an orchard that reflects your current age, what would it look like?

Is there something in the Introduction that you found especially insightful or helpful? Anything you disagree with or would add to what the author has presented?

## I. A Time to Ripen

Has "I am an old person" become a reality for you? What specifics of Elderhood resonate with what you are currently experiencing? How would you describe "Elderhood" to someone forty years younger than yourself?

When did Elderhood begin for you? Have you had a "biggest turn" toward this stage of aging? If so, when did this occur? Are you comfortable with being called "old?"

Where are you in the "ripening" process of older age? What personal qualities or virtues have matured? To which ones would you like to give more thought and attention? (Consider opening a piece of fruit with seeds, holding the seeds in your hand, reflecting on the "seeds" within yourself and how they have developed.)

If you were spoken to in the way the art gallery guard spoke to Donald Hall, how would you respond? Have you experienced ageism, either within yourself or in the way others act toward you? Share an example of this.

Is there something in this chapter that you found especially insightful or helpful? Anything you disagree with or would add to what the author has presented?

## II. Anxiety and Uncertainty

Mention some situations of older persons that elicit resistance, fear, or hesitancy in making choices and decisions. If you've had this kind of emotional response, what took place and what was the end result?

How do you cope with "worrying" and "maintaining an untroubled spirit?" If you were with someone who was overcome with worrying, how would you respond?

Have you ever not done something out of fear or because of a strong concern, and later regretted your decision?

Share a story about something related to older age that prompted a good-sized laugh.

Is there something in this chapter that you found especially insightful or helpful? Anything you disagree with or would add to what the author has presented?

## III. Gifts of Elderhood

The poem "Old Tracks" refers to a personal history composed of experiences that influence who a person becomes. Name four major "steps" that have led you to be the elder you now are.

What do you most value about your age? Of the gifts mentioned in this chapter, which ones do you claim as your own? Are there others not mentioned that you would include?

Marilyn McEntyre suggests that "wisdom rarely, if ever, comes without some suffering." Do you agree? If you are comfortable doing so, share an example of a painful event that influenced one of the beliefs and values that guides your life.

Who are some of your mentors of aging? What qualities of theirs have inspired you in how you choose to live as an older person? What central wisdoms do you want to bequeath to future generations?

Is there something in this chapter that you found especially insightful or helpful? Anything you disagree with or would add to what the author has presented?

## IV. Loss

What have been some of your losses during the past ten years? Which of these has had the greatest impact on you?

Of the people in your life who have died, whom do you especially miss? What in particular do you miss about him or her?

Jane Hirschfield presents old age as a corral closing in. Joyce Rupp pictures increasing diminishment as a depleting pond. What other images could be used to speak about depletion and loss?

When do you experience loneliness? Mary Oliver asks herself if she has "endured loneliness with grace?" How would you respond to her question in regard to yourself?

Is there something in this chapter that you found especially insightful or helpful? Anything you disagree with or would add to what the author has presented?

## V. Grief and Healing

Recall a time of grief and how you managed to move through it. Does what you experienced influence how you are living as an elder? If someone asked you how to heal from non-physical wounding, what would you say?

What are some of your current laments? What tops the list and why did you choose that one?

What are some of your current joys? What tops the list and why did you choose that one?

How well do you extend compassion to yourself? What is most challenging about self-compassion? When have you been most intentional about self-compassion?

Describe one of your regrets. Have you been able to leave it behind?

Is there something in this chapter that you found especially insightful or helpful? Anything you disagree with or would add to what the author has presented?

## VI. Gratitude

Share the story of an experience when you found "the good in the not-so-good." What effect did this have on you?

As you look at your present situation, for what are you most grateful? As you look to the past, what do you especially value in your life's "harvest?"

Of your cherished memories, which ones do you especially enjoy revisiting?

When you think of your "legacy," what comes to mind? What do you desire to pour forth each day from "the chalice of your being"?

Is there something in this chapter that you found especially insightful or helpful? Anything you disagree with or would add to what the author has presented?

## VII. Physical Decline

Of your physical ailments, which one gets most of your attention? What is problematic or challenging for you in regard to how your body is changing?

Take a look at your hands. If they could speak, what might they say? How do you feel about your physical appearance? When you look in the mirror, how would you describe the face looking back at you?

In what ways do you care for your physical and spiritual self? What motivates you to be compassionate toward yourself?

Who or what encourages you to accept the physical decline and increasing limitations that are part of growing older?

Is there something in this chapter that you found especially insightful or helpful? Anything you disagree with or would add to what the author has presented?

## VIII. Death

When you consider your future death, is it a "dreaded enemy," "a liberating guide," or some other notion of a final departure? What would you need to have for yourself in order to attain "a good death?" Is there anything that keeps you from being at peace regarding your mortality?

Comment on Frank Ostaseski's statement, "*Death is the elephant in the room.*" Have you found this to be the case with those you associate with? How and when do you think it is best to speak about human mortality?

What do you think about Thomas Berry's response as to where he will be after he dies? Does this reflect your belief of where you will be after your departure? Do any questions loom large for you when you consider your death? Does religious belief influence how you view your departure?

What are some choices you have made in order to maintain a balance between the reality of future death and entering into your current life as fully as possible?

Is there something in this chapter that you found especially insightful or helpful? Anything you disagree with or would add to what the author has presented?

## IX. Hope and Purpose

Describe your hope. Has it changed as you've gotten older? Do you find hope in one area of your life but not in another part of it? In general, what is the current quality or condition of your hope (steady, weak, strong, quickly dissipates, hard to locate . . . )?

What drains or lessens your hope? With regard to your life, another's, or the condition of the world, have you ever felt like a prairie after it has been scorched?

Who and what sustains your hope? Who are the "unknown angels" who've "come along in your time of need and picked you up?" When have you been an angel for someone else in need of encouragement?

How do you "ache for your life?" Where do you find joy in your day-to-day routine?

What do you see as your purpose in the Elderhood stage? How does this differ from your purpose in the past? Are you at peace with your purpose?

Is there something in this chapter that you found especially insightful or helpful? Anything you disagree with or would add to what the author has presented?

## X. Identity

Reflect on the questions in the third paragraph of "Meeting Mystery in Old Age." Name some of your life-principles and attitudes. Which ones might you be examining? What parts of life remain a mystery for you? How comfortable are you in not having answers, in living with the unknown and the uncertain?

If someone were to ask "Who are you?" what would you say about yourself? Name some of your characteristics and qualities. Do they differ from the characteristics and qualities you had twenty years ago? If you were to design a pattern that demonstrates your current identity, what motif, color, shape, texture, and size would you choose for this design?

Have you, or those you know, experienced some of the characteristics of cognitive impairment? How do you tend to feel and think about changes in the brain as you, or someone you know, ages?

Would you like to "rewild" yourself? If so, how might you do this? What changes would you need to make? What activities would you decide to engage in? What attitudinal adjustments would be required?

Is there something in this chapter that you found especially insightful or helpful? Anything you disagree with or would add to what the author has presented?

## XI. Spiritual Transformation

How would you define "spiritual transformation"? What do you consider to be the basic components of spiritual transformation? Describe one of your significant, transformational experiences.

How are you "coming home" to your authentic self? Which of the images for transformation given in "Polishing the Mirror" most relate to your spiritual growth (fire, sandpaper, stripping, sifting the chaff, a seed's shell splitting off, selling everything, pruning, pickaxe)? Is there a different image you would use?

Recall a time of liminality or darkness in your spiritual growth. What was this like? How did it affect your spirit and the way you now respond to external events?

How are you experiencing "the natural monastery" in your Elderhood years? How comfortable are you with slowing down? Are you at peace with more "be-ing" and less "do-ing?"

Is there something in this chapter that you found especially insightful or helpful? Anything you disagree with or would add to what the author has presented?

## XII. Serenity

How does the principle of detachment affect your aging process? ("Let it go. Let it go. Let it go.") What is most challenging about detachment?

Reflect on (a) a difficult situation when you had no choice except to surrender and (b) another difficult situation when you freely chose to do so. What did you learn from these situations?

When do you especially feel serene or have a sense of peacefulness? What throws your inner stillness off balance? Describe some of the perspectives or spiritual practices that keep your spirit in peace amidst outer turbulence.

How is the aphorism "Love is what counts" influencing your Elderhood years? What are some ways that love travels from your ripened goodness into the lives of others?

Is there something in this chapter that you found especially insightful or helpful? Anything you disagree with or would add to what the author has presented?

## Epilogue—Making the Last Crossing

Which of the four metaphors offered for the final years most relates to your experience—migration, bridge, the interior angel, or the garden sculpture? Is there a different image that you would use? What draws you to choose that particular metaphor?

As you conclude this book and you review and reflect on its content, what aspects stand out for you? Have the topics and content influenced how you will continue to experience your old age? Which areas might you return to from time to time to ponder more fully?

Of the poems in this book, which one(s) particularly spoke to your experience of Elderhood?

If you were asked to summarize your experience of reading and discussing *The Years of Ripening*, what would you say?

Consider closing this final time of reflection on *The Years of Ripening* by having those gathered repeat the four lines of Steven Charleston's at the end of the Epilogue:

*I will not waver in my trust*
*that whatever may come*
*In the end the Spirit of goodness and mercy*
*Will be waiting for me on the other side.*

# Acknowledgments

Books are not written nor are they successful without the support and assistance of dedicated, caring individuals. Here are some of the many to whom I am indebted.

Gracious publisher Robert Ellsberg and the Orbis Books staff, especially Celine Allen, Maria Angelini, Bernadette Price, and Wanda Rodriquez. My Servite friend, Val Lewandoski, who gave large amounts of her time to read and edit the text. Mary Powell led me to the image of ripening in regard to the aging process.

I owe much gratitude to family, friends, and colleagues, for their encouraging presence and the insights I gained from those who responded to my interview questionnaire: Jim Adamson, Janet Barnes, Tim and Trudy Barry, Bobbi Bussan O.S.B., Tina Cafaro, Jerry and Lois Schallau Chettinger, Kathy Coffey, Karen Massingale Ewan, Jean Deliganis, Don and Marilyn Duwelius, Mary Ferring, Rev. Wm Fitzgerald, Charlotte Huetteman O.S.M., Jim and Melinda Jackson, Peg Madigan, Nancy Marsh O.S.M., Margaret McAvity, Jim O'Halloran, Kevin Pokorny, Norma Phelan, John Pollard, Judy Porter, Austin Repath, Rose Roeder, Jerry and Melanie Rupp, Art and Margaret Ann Schmidt, Mary Southard, Carol Thomsen, Jo Tuttle, Renee Sernett Visness, Kim Voyle, John and Carmen Lampe Zeitler.

The sisters in my Servite community have been generous with their support, especially those in leadership and members of the *Elderhood Explorers* group: Prioresses Jackie Ryan and Lisa Sheridan, Lucille Beaulieu, Mary Peter Caito, Iris DePrez, Angeline Hakel, Mary Alice Haley, Mary Hogan, Imelda Kirkey, Rita Kolbert, Ann Moran, Terese Lux, Suzanne Vandenheede, and Zita Sharrow.

A special thanks to you, my faithful readers. You help me believe in the worth of my writing and sustain my confidence to continue.